THE FULLNESS OF TIME

First published in 2010 by
The Dedalus Press
13 Moyclare Road
Baldoyle
Dublin 13
Ireland

www.dedaluspress.com

Copyright © Gerard Smyth, 2010

ISBN 978 1 906614 26 3 (hardbound)
ISBN 978 1 906614 27 0 (paperback)

All rights reserved.
No part of this publication may be reproduced in any form or by any means without the prior permission of the publisher.

Dedalus Press titles are represented in North America by Syracuse University Press, Inc., 621 Skytop Road, Suite 110, Syracuse, New York 13244, and in the UK by Central Books, 99 Wallis Road, London E9 5LN

Cover image © Karl Smyth

The Dedalus Press receives financial assistance from
The Arts Council / An Chomhairle Ealaíon

THE FULLNESS OF TIME
NEW AND SELECTED POEMS

Gerard Smyth

With an Introduction by
Thomas McCarthy

DEDALUS PRESS
DUBLIN, IRELAND

ACKNOWLEDGEMENTS

Acknowledgements are due to the editors of the following publications in which some of these poems first appeared: *Agenda, Best Irish Poetry (2008 and 2010), Blue Canary (Milwaukee), Boulevard Magenta, Cork Literary Review, Cyphers, Irish Pages, Poetry Europe* (Journal of the European Academy of Poetry), *Poetry Ireland Review, Poetry London, Salamander* (Boston), *Southword, The SHOp, The Stony Thursday Book, The Irish Times, The Warwick Review, Waxwing Poems, Notes From His Contemporaries: A Tribute to Michael Hartnett,* and on the online sites, *Poetry Daily, Poetry International* and *Southword Online.*

Also in the anthologies *Night and Day: Twenty Four Hours in the Life of Dublin City* (edited by Dermot Bolger), *Our Shared Japan* (edited by Irene de Angelis and Joseph Woods), *Sunday Miscellany* (edited by Cliodhna Ní Anluain) and *A Treasury of Sunday Miscellany* (edited by Marie Heaney).

Several of the poems were broadcast on the RTÉ Radio programmes Sunday Miscellany and The Arts Show. 'Blue Crucifixion' appeared in the catalogue for the Hughie O'Donoghue exhibition, Recent Paintings and Selected Works from the American Ireland Fund Donation, in the Irish Museum of Modern Art in March-May 2009.

Poems in the Selected sections were previously published in *The Flags are Quiet* (New Writers' Press, 1969), *Orchestra of Silence* (Tara Telephone, 1971), *World Without End* (New Writers' Press, 1977), *Loss and Gain* (Raven Arts Press, 1981), *Painting the Pink Roses Black* (Dedalus Press, 1986), *Daytime Sleeper* (Dedalus Press, 2002), *A New Tenancy* (Dedalus Press, 2004) and *The Mirror Tent* (Dedalus Press, 2007). Several of these poems have been revised for this collection.

For Pauline

Contents

INTRODUCTION by Thomas McCarthy / xiii

NEW POEMS

THE FULLNESS OF TIME / 1

A Memory / 5
With the Dreamers / 6
Ancestor / 7
Lambs / 8
Shop of Cures / 9
Parlour Ballad / 10
Early Anecdote / 11
Marbles / 12
Winter Clock / 13
Lost Photograph / 14
Luther's People / 15
Sixth Day / 16
In the Eblana Bookshop / 17
In the Brazen Head / 18
One Evening After Songs of Praise / 19
Smoke / 20
Nightsong / 21
Ark / 22
Evenings in the Rocking Chair / 23
Late in Life / 24
Covenant / 25
The Unease of Clouds / 26
The Holly Wreath is Dead… / 27
Belief / 28

Nicodemus / 29
Blue Crucifixion / 30
Blackbird / 31
December Moon / 32
Saginaw / 33
Heinrich Böll on Achill / 34
To the Wedding / 35
Paris Before Colour Photography / 36
Luxembourg Gardens / 37
Galilee / 38
No Infidels / 39
A Different America / 40
To Ludgate Hill / 41
Seen and Heard / 42
My Father's Hat / 44
Elegy for James / 45
Fellini's Dreams / 46
Ars Poetica / 47
Tomorrow's Stanzas / 48
To a Genealogist / 49
Souvenirs of Hard Times / 50

SELECTED POEMS

1

Today is Not Enough / 55
Evensong / 56
Yard / 57
Childhood House / 59
Dollars / 60
Smokehouse / 61
The Black Kettle Singing / 62

The Old Life / 63
Daguerreotype / 65
Hen Woman / 66
Squeeze Box / 67
Arcadia / 68
Ancestral Place / 69
Dreamsong / 70

2

April Love Poem / 73
The Forty Steps / 74
Amsterdam / 75
You And I / 76
Comforter / 77
Dedications / 78
Surrender / 79
Cool of the Day / 80
Last Star Smouldering / 81
Everyday Life / 82
Housewarming / 84
Vladimir Holan was Right / 85
A New Tenancy / 86

3

All That is Left / 89
Return / 90
T.K.'s Territory / 91
Portobello Bridge / 92
Terra Cognita / 93
Survivors / 94
Draper's Window / 95
In the Bakery / 96

Sam's Junkshop / 97
River Gulls and City Horses / 98
Fifties Child / 100
Carnival / 101
Picturehouse / 102
Mid-Century Sunday / 103
Postscript / 104
Written From Memory / 105
An Evening Walk in Maryland / 106
The Hot Bread of St. Catherine's / 107
Hartmann's Camera / 108
Eccles Street / 109
Songs in Sepia / 110
High Windows / 111
Family Lore / 112
Shanty / 114
Armistice / 115
Gas Mask / 116
After Many Years / 117
Finger-Writing on Window Dust / 118
The Long Afternoon / 119
Riddles and Orisons / 120
Girl in Blue Denim / 121
A Previous Life / 122
The Cana Inn / 123
Same Old Crowd / 124

4

The Solitary Life / 127
He Who Treads The Boards / 128
Epiphany / 129
Comet / 130
Two Stops on the Way to the Sea / 131
Mangan / 133

Homage to Hartnett / 134
An Abstract Life / 135
Ezra / 136
Hopkins / 137
Lorca / 138
Georg Trakl / 139
Lives of the Artists / 140
Night in St. Cloud / 143
Club Nocturne / 144
Whiskey Bar on Moonlight Drive / 146
Golden Lane / 147
Visiting Chopin's Heart / 148
The Calling Angel / 149
Elysian Colours / 150
St. Petersburg Triptych / 151
About the Wounds / 153
To a Latvian Poet / 154
In Vilnius / 155
Jan Palach / 156
Villa Florica / 157
Sunday Morning in Romania / 158
Haunts / 159
Museum of Last Things / 160
Snapshots / 161
Sagrada Familia / 162
Celtic Landscape / 163
Cross of Moone / 164
Glendalough / 165
Boyne Tomb / 166
Achill / 167
Paperweight / 168
The History of Fog / 169
Wonderland / 170
Sea Pictures / 172
Surrogate / 174
Flood / 175

Spirit of the Fireman / 176
In God's Ballroom / 177
Elegy for Caesar / 178
According to Matthew / 179
Interlude / 180
Lough Derg / 181
World Without End / 182
Creed Room / 183
Daytime Sleeper / 184
Pink Roses Black / 185
The Mirror Tent / 186
Poem Beginning with a Line from Raymond Carver / 187
Gifts / 188
Corrib / 189
Nora Barnacle's House / 190
September Song / 191
Free State / 192
Goldenbridge / 193
Aria / 194
Elegy in March / 195
End of Story / 196
Ovid in the Garden / 197
Putting on the Grey Suit / 198

Introduction

At the heart of Gerard Smyth's entire oeuvre is an intriguing duality. He is an urban poet who emerged as an artist from the distinctive Dublin modernism of Michael Smith's New Writers' Press, yet his work over the years has accumulated all the characteristics of a compelling, Kavanagh-like, story-telling narrative method. In sensibility and world view he is entirely modernist, but he has layered a classically Irish story-teller fixative upon the canvas of urbane, ironic sensibilities.

In the late Sixties and early Seventies New Writers' Press published *The Flags are Quiet* and *Twenty Poems*, while the youthful, modernist Tara Telephone published *Orchestra of Silence*. This was minimalist poetry, praised by the author of *Anatomy of a Cliché*, Michael Hartnett, who argued that Smyth would go on to do in poetry what Joyce had done for Dublin in prose. Shortly before his death, James Liddy called Smyth "the chronicler of Irish life." Gerard Smyth's aesthetic, a reticent tone that signifies a disciple of ironic internationalism, also signalled an attachment to place and parish and named locale. The trenchant, Kinsella-like description of 'Yard':

> A zinc bucket rattles the wind.
> And billowing like a length of silk
> A nettlebed crowns the golden dungheap.

Or the house in 'A New Tenancy':

> brass and brick and balustrades
> that split the late sun at evening
> as it filtered through skylight glass

are aesthetic signals that here we have a poet used to cobble-stones, courtyards and Estella Solomons' shadows. Dublin is Smyth's synagogue, the place of worship and living symbol of something semi-detached from the bog-trotting story time of the world beyond electric lights. Here is a poet who might have walked from theatre to theatre with Con Leventhal or a young Beckett. In 'Sam's Junkshop' he shows us

> A display of dross: the strange,
> the familiar: mouth organ, jew's harp.
>
> Like a character out of Isaac Bashevis Singer,
> he stood in the doorway,
> his bulk blocking the entrance to the muddle
> of disowned and unwanted possessions.

While in 'Written From Memory' he gives us the wise and taciturn milk wagons, bakers' vans, convent bells and men in crumpled clothes. He recreates his father's "city of lore" in 'Hartmann's Camera' as well as the hot bread prepared for tradesmen and apprentices; and the cures

> concocted by Mushatt the chemist,
> the hot bread of St. Catherine's.

It is 1950s Dublin and the more Joycean "silver age of the sepia print" of 'Eccles Street.' The sinister places are not forgotten, either, in the dark geography of 'Goldenbridge:'

> Leaving behind all you loved—
> you stepped into the glimmer-world
> of orphanage and sanatorium,
> dormitory and TB room:
> places so well hidden
> they could have been the hidden half of the moon.

But it is Dublin geography, a compelling Dublin remembered but washed clean of sentimentality like the wet cobble-stones of St. James's Gate, a landscape first balanced for our own generation in the theodolite of Thomas Kinsella, that Smyth has collected into a personal myth kitty and word hoard. Inheritor of that cobble-stoned living, Smyth has indeed loitered in a unique Dublin neighbourhood of modernism. In his poems are the polished shoes that forever await their Sabbath. Memories are put away like folded wings and the clickety-clack of his poetic sewing-machine trembles across every page in the *Selected*. It is Dublin, most certainly, that calls him to account, as in the wayfarer in 'Portobello Bridge'

> When I first came to the footbridge
> at the lock, as a child
> with fishing net and pinkeen pot,
> it was through Little Jerusalem:
> the avenues of exile,
> past the synagogue that is now the mosque.

Dublin made him the poet he is, that is certainly true. But there are other aspects of his work worth remarking upon, especially now that we have the pleasure of a major assembly of the work in this book. There are many journeys in this poetry, journeys away from Dublin, beyond St. Patrick's Clock and Portobello Bridge. Firstly, there's the inner journey into domestic life, romance and fatherhood, and a steady accumulation of generations through both marriage and memory. In 'Housewarming' he writes

> For luck we brought a nugget of coal
> and salt: the double talisman
> to protect our four walls and fire-hearth

while in 'Cool of the Day' he writes "Her face has always been the iconography / of my best dreams: my gladness, / my rapture, my golden apple." What began in 'A New Tenancy' has been sustained through the crowded rooms of poetry. There is an uncanny, risking certainty in these poems of family and generations; a sense of warm interior in contrast to the social and physical cold outside. In 'Evenings in the Rocking Chair' he celebrates the youthfulness of love with all the confidence of the settled and the truly loved:

> We raise a glass, remembering our long good-byes
> in the shadow that fell from the clock-tower
> of the Church of St. Catherine.

He moves back and forth through that home-centred lens, from the memory of his father reading to the gradual withdrawal of his own children into maturity and individuality. But Smyth is a daily wordsmith, a writer and editor in the hardest territory: the daily newspaper. It is hardly surprising that part of the iconography of his love, domestic and romantic, are those talismans of published poetry, the sacred medallions and votive offerings of books. In 'A Previous Life' the beloved is left under no illusion but that her lover is a literary lover:

> Your kiss was then a healing art
> after the dance, under the trees
> on Clanbrassil Street,
> the corner where in an ardent
>
> trance we drew close
> and I placed in your hands
> the gospel of Pablo Neruda.
> His twenty love poems and song of despair.

Even in the arc of love the published, literary companions are placed across the firmament in a comforting rainbow. And this is the aspect of Gerard Smyth's work that should not be overlooked—here is a literary poet, not a memoirist of inner city life, not just an auto-biographer pulling fiercely, instinctively, against the ironies of modernism and the trenchant minimalism of young Hartnett or Michael Smith, or the ancestral poetries of Beckett, Coffey or even Con Leventhal's beloved, Ethna MacCarthy. Here is a literary creature, a reader, an editor, a wanderer in other poetries. There is more to this poet than Palgrave's Treasury or the remnants of liturgical sayings and hymns. Here is a poet who has sought company and instruction, who has made daily decisions about the word itself and negotiated in a territory seeded with published volumes and books awaiting review.

Many of the poems in this *Selected* insert flags of recognition through the geography of life-long reading: "So, this is poetry,' I said/ on my journey with the *Nightwalker*." In the Eblana bookshop, no doubt escaping at lunchtime from the hot type of the newspaper office, the poet invokes Kinsella, Mandelstam, Machado and Neruda. In later poems we visit Roethke's Saginaw valley, with its lost son gone for good, and Heinrich Böll on Achill:

> looking for answers in a deserted village,
> in the wet winds that battered your sanctuary,
>
> the warmed-up cottage on the hill.

There is a whole host of elders invoked here, icons of style and dedication. We journey to Frost's New England, Ann Frank's Amsterdam, Yeats' Drumcliff and Lissadell, as well as Hopkins arriving, not at a country, but at a piece of music by Purcell. The poet has resolutely set himself down among the lilies of the field, the almost familial and filial field of international poets. Like any true modernist, Smyth has trust in the common humanity of foreigners, a belief in the redemption of brief encounters. He draws solace from the certainty of having received wisdom from poets who might have appeared indifferently distant from the cobblestones of inner Dublin. We journey to "Granada where the stones / were simmering in the heat / and flowers were withering / to ghost flowers / in Manuel de Falla's house" as well as to the commonplace office where:

> We write reports and pass away a life
> as foot-soldiers making footnotes,
> field-workers among the sheaves
>
> counting down the office hours,
> the middle years
> until they reach the last hour ….

This is from 'Putting on the Grey Suit' a poem dedicated to Dennis O'Driscoll, a fellow wage-slave and poet who tries to keep the flame of poetry alive in the quotidian darkness of the office. O'Driscoll, like Smyth, has always had ears tuned to faraway signals, signals of poetic life in North and Eastern Europe: such sensitivity creates a new music in Irish poetry. Knowledge of what has happened elsewhere, a pity for that struggle which may never be translated, is part of the underlying, anxious rhythms of Smyth's earliest poetry. This fellow feeling, a recognition of the burdens others carry for poetry, is also seen in 'Mangan' and 'Homage to Hartnett:'

> When the blackbird whistled
> in the school-hedge hedges
> of Croom and Camas
> he was there to listen, a naturalist,
> a new and living Ó Rathaile.

A poem like 'Sea Pictures' creates another transition within this *Selected*: this house of sea pictures draws attention to what is a very effective suite of poems on painters and paintings. Visual art is one of the toll roads through the Smyth landscape, and the poet here pays his way by constant homage and praise.

In 'Wonderland' the artist Sean McSweeney paints 'the ephemeral haze/ of a sky in the west, works the spell that makes/ the wetland pool a window to the underearth—

> The artist as eulogist scans the landscape,
> its tones and tints: nimbus, spindrift,
> the mountain slope of rock and stone.

In 'St. Petersburg Triptych' he pays homage to the 'honeyed and opulent' amber of the Baltic, finding himself within Akhmatova's courtyard and, later, standing before "The doomsday book... open / at a page inscribed in *bas-relief*." In 'Elysian Colours,' written after watching Tarkovsky's *Andrei Rublev*, he emphasises

> The conversation with Theophanes
> who called him to his side,
> who taught him how to trace the first outline
> and paint with Elysian colours
> the Byzantine Christ.

Here are assembled Fellini's dreams, Van Gogh and Goya, an appointment with the flowers of Georgia O'Keeffe, Delacroix, Bonnard, Rothko and Giotto, his Virgin "blue-robed and beautiful / even with the cracks of centuries blemishing her features." It is an aesthetic assemblage, Art named and numbered "as if a thief had taken your thoughts." Art here, high Art, is familiar as cobblestones and as central as family and domestic love.

This is a generous selection, from poet and publisher, evidence of a honeyed and opulent imagination. Here is a poet alright, and Dublin made him.

—Thomas McCarthy

The Fullness of Time

In unframed pictures of the fullness of time
I am younger, older, sometimes
an age that cannot be guessed.
Winter into spring, autumn after summer—
to count the years of recent history
I begin at mother's breast,
then see myself on father's shoulder
that year he wore cloth of herring-bone.

First lessons at the inkwell,
the primer open, the pencil sharpened,
then the mantra that's good for the soul
recited like a Greek chorus.
In unframed pictures of the fullness of time
I am a child on sand building a castle
that's swept away by the sea's advance,
a tide that out-sings all of nature.

As a child of the parish, I am told to stray
no farther than the streets I know by name.
I am fresh-faced but soon wearing the first trace
of a boy-to-manhood beard, my snowy mask
of middle years when I begin to glimpse
in my mirror-image the ghost of my father,
not looking old but as he appeared
that year he wore cloth of herring-bone.

NEW POEMS

A Memory

In her apron pockets she kept
hair clips, fag-ends, Emerald sweets.
This woman fettered to a small farm:
its vigils, its seasons of digging and cutting,
gathering in, storing up.

In the cow parlour, in the chill of daybreak,
in the slant of evening sun,
the three-legged stool was the throne she sat on.
Milk hitting the bucket of white enamel
made oracular music.

All afternoon the aria of a common bird
came from the shaded wood.
In the house with walls of clay mud,
she kept the peat-fire burning and made the meal
to fatten the pigs: old turnips and fermented milk.

With the Dreamers

Outside in the yard there were different rhythms:
the old hen scratching the dung-cairn,
the swish of willows like a slight rebuke.

Flicking through the wavebands, looking for Raidió Éireann
we came upon a country singer's song of yearning,
Roy Orbison's falsetto.

The roads that afternoon were melting to a high gloss.
While the new hay was turned and tossed
I was indoors with the dreamers,

up in the room at the gable-end
where the little lamp that was part of the night
left scorch-marks on the ceiling.

I was listening to bread being kneaded
and keeping watch for the neighbour who always appeared
from across the fields, through a gap in Eden.

Ancestor

The nail in the wall that a horseshoe hangs on
was put there, hammered in
by an ancestor who never envisaged
how his saplings would flourish
from supple branches to strong sinews
or how his virgin grass would become an idyll
for a city child in summer months.

Ancestor who knew how to sing
when the black liquid crossed your lips.
Ploughman who put on his smile
to pause for the time it took to create
this blurred image that I hold to the light
to see the resemblance seeded in my own visage.

Lambs

On an evening that showed me once
how the end of August comes to sadden us,
I gathered up the fallen cones
in the corner of the yard,
in the shadow of the willow.
Then I walked as far as the thistle-field,
the stream without a ripple.
Along the track of indentations in the grass
to the place where cattle came to drink
from their reflections, and I to think.
I had questions to ask and all the answers
shook the branches of the trees,
made the hinges creak
on that old gate that locked us out, locked us in.
In the slaughterhouse lambs
were waiting, knives prepared
for the village butcher whose *coup de grace*
took half a minute. I remember him still,
slightly stooped, red-faced grin,
his apron like a pelt around him.
His black Wellingtons ankle-deep in entrails

Shop of Cures

They came with their afflictions to the shop of cures:
those in need of small mercies, or small miracles.
Some with fire in their throats, an ache in their bones,
with ailments, agonies, a rasp in their chests.

Like sorcerer and apprentice, the apothecaries
in mint white coats, kept to their side of the counter
among the remedies, spooning powders into the mix,
deciphering the medicine scripts.

They came with their shivers, crowds of the sick
crowding into the cramped space between glass jars
of glucose sticks, iron for the blood,
into the presence of those high priests who knew by heart

where to reach for wart-cures, cough mixtures,
preparations that tasted sweet,
ointments that had to be rubbed on, rubbed in,
that radiated the balm of healing.

Parlour Ballad

for Ethel and Joe Smith

They were not to be touched, the wedding gifts
in the front parlours of childhood.
China dogs, candlesticks; seashells which
if we held them to our ears
let us hear a faint sea-prayer.

That room, a sanctum we tiptoed through
with its woodshine, lampglow,
was where the grown-ups sat together
on the sofa or stood at the window
looking out through lace curtains.

It was where we were sent
when we did not show respect. On the mantle
family relics were always immaculate
after the once-over with the rag.

There the clans of inter-marriage gathered:
pipe-smokers oozing the pungency
of strong tobacco; sisters who saw the future
simply by looking into their cups
at what the cold tea-dust revealed: a journey
across the sea, good luck, ill-omen, money.

Early Anecdote

In Januaries of snow, Junes of harvest weather
school years passed like a carnival parade.

It was still the age of pen and paper
and the movie poster for *Lawrence of Arabia.*

Through backstreets behind the brewery
my snow-prints followed me, turning corners,

slogging along or stopping when I stopped
in the granite shade of hopstore walls

those mornings when I headed off, hurrying
to reach the yard before the hand-bell made its call.

Carrying in my bag the tattered atlas
and the narrative of Caesar's war in Gaul.

Marbles

Playing marbles in the avenue.
I loved their colours rolling on the path,
the spherical motion, the smack
when glass hit glass. We had fistfuls of them,
collections stashed in cloth bags
that we clutched like a treasure chest.
We exchanged and traded them.
Bluebottle blues for bloodshot reds.
It was part of the camaraderie of boys back then.
Kaleidoscopic, polished to the lustre of a gem,
sometimes they'd spill and fall,
pirouetting in all directions, slipping through
the grill and down the rain-shore.
A loss for which there was no consolation.

Winter Clock

On a wintry morning, in the intermission
between two seasons,
and just before the winter clock
darkened our evenings, I was a child agog

at the moments of stillness
when her coffin was hoisted
on the shoulders of men
whose shoulders were dependable,

when up in the tangle of quivering branches
prayers were snagged
on their way to heaven's army
of prayer-catchers, and my father

shouldered the drops of rain
that fell on him and became his mask.
Then turned for home, to his test of faith—
the solitude of the patriarch.

Lost Photograph

The gentle ones, the lord of mockery with his grin,
the torturer and the torturer's victim.
I recognise them: the boys in the school photograph
as they were then, with their long hair,
first nicks of the razor.

The tall and gangly, the barrel-chested.
Some had good looks, some the attributes
of mysteriousness. When I try to recall
the nomenclature, their names go missing:
The boys in the school photograph
who wear submissive expressions.

They stand side by side—smiles and scowls
and formal gestures. They stare blankly,
look straight ahead—seeing nothing
of what the future held, thinking only of tomorrow's
matinée: the double-bill of happy endings.

Luther's People

As children not much older than the age of reason,
there was a place we never dared to enter.
Our elders whispered about half-believers,
strange priest-craft, Luther's people.
That the bread in there was only bread
and not the flesh of the Redeemer.

Inside the cathedral, light was needed
to reveal the pages of the hymn-book and the bible.
The boy sopranos were harmonising
a rebuke to vanity, a rebuke to pride:
holy verses handed down through the tribe.
Their wore their choir-gowns like a birthright,
a heritage, and mustered themselves in rows
between flag-emblems from the Book of Heraldry.

Sixth Day

The stonemason labouring with the wings of an angel
heard the shriek of gulls like a battle raging
over the river: the worried face of Anna Livia.

It was Saturday morning, birds in cages were out in the sun.
No other day of the week was so full of talk in the streets,
folk-wisdom under awnings shading bread and meat.

Ignoring what was said to the rich young man told
to relinquish all he possessed, the shopkeepers
stood as close as they could to their cash registers.

The bells of the parishes cast bell-harmonies
on the last breeze of September.
In streets where the wanderer could wander forever

the street musician knew which song could still the crowd,
make them feel pity and spill from their pockets
loose change like afterthoughts to his borrowed refrains.

In the Eblana Bookshop

The bell above the door tinkled
when I entered, tinkled when I left.
A book in the big window
cast a spell and called me in
to the poets' cradle in the corner.
'So this is poetry', I said
on my journey with the *Nightwalker*.

And Mandelstam, *O Mandelstam*,
your spirit moved in that spirit world
too, where there was no sound
except the brush that swept
the wooden floor and pages turning.
And because the natural light
grew dim, there were lights turned on
in the afternoon. I was a novice
Prospero—gone astray,
lost in stanzas and storybook chapters,
there for the solitary pleasure of loitering
where time stood still in the gap
between Machado and Neruda.

In the Brazen Head

Under the image of the rebel on the scaffold,
perhaps on the very spot where the plot was hatched,
we sat in a corner of the Brazen Head,
spent long evenings until we came to the dregs,
sharing the company of men of all trades,
fellow-travellers in from the cold, in from the rain,
from nights of frost and the four winds passing
through places soon to be rubble, sites of desecration.
We sat in a Cupid's corner, eavesdropping
on raw music in the backroom: banjo and whistle,
and the balladeers swilling songs
from the cup of tradition: *Boulevogue, The Foggy Dew.*
All the listeners keeping time, tapping the tunes.

One Evening After Songs of Praise

It was our first home, built on ground
that belonged to ghosts,
on a height that in January caught the first snows,
that in June came alive when it became
a place for outings on golden evenings,
for *hide-and-seek* and *finders keepers*.

The house settled, absorbed new sounds:
a stereo playing *New Kid in Town*,
the easeful kettle coming to the boil,
banging doors, rattle of cups,
our firstborn speaking first words in his high chair.

One evening after Songs of Praise
I stepped out into the cul-de-sac,
lifted my gaze
and saw the lights come on in upper windows,
the glow of televisions.
Out of the dusk-fragrance, the eerie calm,
a voice called the names of children lingering
in one last game of *catch-me-if-you-can*.

Smoke

Languorously it poured,
the smoke from our city fires:
the strong blaze, the smouldering embers.
Smoke from factories, from homes,
from the brazier of the night-watchman,
the funnel of the ship unloading
at the mouth of the river.

Once it was everywhere and sulphurous,
hiding our city's shame, billowing upwards
from the stoked furnace
to make the sky a ferment of murky-colours
as if the end of the world was coming.
It alarmed the birds on rooftop aerials,
fouled the vistas of a city in decay.

Rising from boiler-house chimneys
it was an afterlife tossed away by river-wind
that made its own music: sometimes a nocturne,
sometimes a Wagnerian tempest of sound.
It vanished without ceremony,
the way all things do—matter and spirit,
time and the places that time passed through.

Nightsong

For many nights I stayed awake
with the typographer setting the pages
of the first edition, keeping vigil
for fires and floods, what might be news
or might go down in history.

It was always late when I walked the thoroughfare
that was like a shipyard with no ships.
Always late when I met the midwife
going home from doing what she did
among the new-born or saw lights flicked on
in the Seaman's Mission,
for someone there to check the almanac of tides.

The milkman rattled his pints of milk.
The office cleaners wiped the stains,
removed the dust, did their dawn-work in the hush
of the Ship of State, and the emporium
with its glass doors shut and its "Closed" sign turned
to face the sleeper in the doorway.

Ark

for my sister Anne

The ark that sheltered us submits to ruin,
neglect, abandonment. There's a ghostly ambience
where chattels have vanished, where mornings
of motherhood had their own chronology.

It happens by stealth: the ark that sheltered us
becomes a remnant of the past, unroofed, stripped bare
as if a thief passed through it taking everything
but the black shadows, the creak on the stair.

Doors are padlocked to their frames—
doors to which contagion came
to give the loudest knock: scarlet fever, whooping cough.

That familiar room where time has stopped,
was birth-place, sickbay, nursery—a zone of memory
behind frosted glass. Light from street-lamps

shone in at night illuminating folded garments,
household objects; the butter, golden in its dish,
the stove-lid blackened with a rub of polish.

Evenings in the Rocking Chair

A Valentine for P

These are good days that end with evenings
in the rocking chair, raising a glass
to that far-off April in the discotheque of chance,
or strolling the Fifteen Acres, its beds of grass cradling us.
We raise a glass, remembering our long good-byes
in the shadow that fell from the clock-tower
of the Church of St. Catherine.
Gulls circling overhead and always one of them
crying like nobody's child.

These are good days that end with evenings
in the rocking chair, when sometimes we seem
like a ghost-semblance of what we were that Whitsuntide
we knelt on the marble steps and the nuptial prayer
passed over us through the motes of dust
rising upwards, like woken spirits in the shafts of sunlight.

Late in Life

Late in life we come back to the waves at Achill,
to hear again the sounds they made
on our first nights of marriage.

We come back to where the sky waters the earth,
to retrace our steps on the road we trudged
like pilgrims on a pilgrim-quest,

or on which we hurried with the haste
of lovers to their beds. We come back to walk
the gauntlet of fuchsia bells, to where swifts

and swallows out of nowhere or blown off course
go with speed like fugitives into the Valley
of the Cuckoo, over the headland of gorse.

We come back to see again the raw light of the west,
to the stillness of the charred bog, to where sea-fog
edges slowly through the graveyard without walls

where rain is gathering, wind bites hard
and twilight gives sanctuary to those who pray
that their prayers will be answered.

Covenant

for David Gardiner

Southbound to Coolgreany weather slowed our journey time.
It seemed as if judgment was upon us, that high trees
could be drowned. The road became a tributary

of frothing streams when rain from clouds of mourning fell,
a downpour so masculine and minatory it was a sky-god's revenge
on the sun. The oceans of heaven were emptying

into the rivers of Wexford, into some cuckoo's nest.
Then a rainbow like a sign in the firmament stood rigged
between two vales of foliage, grass and ferns.

When a second rainbow crowned the first, more perfect one
we saw before us an arch of circus colours,
keeping its distance, its old mystique made new again.

The Unease of Clouds

The unease of clouds
is there to see in the sky that touches
Three Rock Mountain. Last night we heard
the weatherman's announcement that hearts would freeze
in the falling temperatures, the blast of the easterlies.

This, as Bly in one of his snow-poems says,
is *the sort of snowfall that starts in late afternoon*
when the sky is crepuscular and threatening,
sending soft flurries at first,
then the heavier stuff like a pointillist's spectacle.

To the hillsides of myrtle and walls of the prisons,
it brings the glow of the Far North,
the solemnity of the shadow of the Cross,
this snow that sweeps into foxholes,
that blows through the bogs, making everything abstract.

The Holly Wreath is Dead...

The holly wreath is dead in the Christmas rubbish.
The old calendar has no more days to give us.
There is the usual percussion of car-locks opening, shutting.
The early riser left his house in the chill before the sun came out
to thaw the night-frost on the cars and the silver blades of grass.
On the path that must be followed, sons and daughters
dawdle to the backbeat of their Walkman-tunes.
They have questions to ask about the murdered and the missing,
about the wars they see on the news.
And sometimes too about the God of their religion.

Belief

Last Easter in the sun-warmed chapel
through Harry Clarke's stained-glass
window of The Passion
the rays of light reached down
to touch the Scriptures, open on the page
where the women came
to find the stone rolled back,
the empty graveclothes in a heap.
A scene to baffle the grieving Marys.
The end and the beginning of Belief.

Nicodemus

After the Good Friday ceremony,
the wooden cross without a Christ,
I think of Nicodemus, his night-visits

and how I too am secretive
about the appointments I keep,
always, it seems, in that place

where we go for forgiveness;
the sanctuary described by R.S. Thomas
as *the ante-room of the spirit.*

Blue Crucifixion

for Clare and Hughie O'Donoghue

Not the crudely sketched
man of sorrows
from the cover-image
of the old school catechism
that was touched
and smudged so much
it lost its mystic fragrance.

And not Gauguin's Yellow Christ
in the Breton countryside,
a Golgotha made strange
by those maids in attendance.
Or Poussin's Redeemer
down from the Cross
under the gaze of the spellbound.

But the Blue Crucifixion
shows a fleshy semblance
of human wreckage that belongs
to a man who was *counted
among the transgressors.*
Our idea of him electrified
by such mystery as art requires.

Blackbird

Our blackbird has haunted us
with his summer of song.
And now we cannot imagine him gone
with his wake-up call and long serenade,
constant since we turned back
the clock in April.

In the green lustre
of the tree outside the kitchen
his chatter was like a monologue
of reminiscence. His song of songs
we heard, often before daybreak
more often as our evening entertainment.

Once there were two of them,
with their call and answer: the Peeping Tom
well hidden in the bushes,
the worm-gatherer out front, showing courage.

December Moon

The December moon like an alabaster mask
lords it over the long night.
It illuminates the gravel path,
looks into the bedroom mirror
and leaves its cold breath there.

A moon that lights weed-covered yards
and the ruins of Clonmacnoise.
It is chained to the hours of slow time,
creeps through temple and church,
and knows where the crime was done.

It shines into the cradle,
appears through rain in the cemetery:
same orb that Bashō saw
in his garden, above the cherry-tree.

Saginaw

In Saginaw, under the metropolitan clocks,
he wandered, humming a waltz
his father taught him. It was nowhere spectacular:
a town where the pace was slow,
with its drive-in, drug store, funeral parlour,
whine of saws in the lumber factory.

It was where he became a lord of nature,
a mind in disrepair, a companion
to whatever crawled under the rocks,
to tendrils and weeds in the flower-beds,
long stems with their blossoms of scent.

Set free from his father's house
with its festivals of second flowering,
he became a lost son gone for good, flanked
by his own big shadow on the highway to Parnassus,
off to a life of psalms, a life abandoned to chance.

Heinrich Böll on Achill

As Soyinka says
They varied death a thousand ways.

You would have understood that phrase.
You who came to these valleys

dipped in mountain-shadows,
to hear the bleating of lambs

from scrawny pastures, see how dark
the night can be and how bewitching

the galaxies over bog and bay,
decaying harbour, stony vista.

Was it for the bliss of a life far from Troy's
battle hymns you came: True witness

looking for answers in a deserted village,
in the wet winds that battered your sanctuary,

the warmed-up cottage on the hill.
That was how your storm days passed on Achill.

To the Wedding

Twice we crossed the Shannon
and twice we passed close to King John's Castle.
All in one day there was a blessing,
a feast, the gaiety of a wedding in full swing.

The jingle-jangle of a hit song faded out, faded in.
A fiddle and tin whistle began serenely
but soon they soared: rampant, voluble.
Every dancer dropping the sweat of rapture.

Earlier in the little hillside chapel,
looking up I noticed that the Crucifixion scene
was almost palpable above the maids of honour
kneeling down on satin pillows.

Paris Before Colour Photography

They queue to enter the honeycomb of the Louvre
to view Delacroix's flag and *The Raft of the Medusa*.
Or Giotto's Virgin, blue-robed and beautiful
even with the cracks of centuries blemishing her features.
They have come to Paris in its yellow season
of fat pigeons and cemetery leaves falling like ballerinas
in Montparnasse. The river puts on a show
of river traffic: pleasure boats whose passengers see Paris
as it was before colour photography.
A bitter breeze blows through Rue Descartes
and those streets where the bells of St. Genevieve
were first to speak when the prince of poets
calling for the last sacrament
slipped the leash of Paris without a backward glance.

Luxembourg Gardens

Here in the Luxembourg Gardens
there are leaves to be gathered
and petals from the flowers of France.

There's a new transparency
that the time of blossoming lacked.
And perpetual motion: Sunday joggers

shuffling the gravel, running in circles
for the sake of their hearts.
Those at ease cast pallid shadows:

the blind man with cane and Labrador,
the book lover on the last chapter of Balzac.
Avenue and arbour, haunt of the flaneur

who walks in idle bliss on the way
to the Palace of Justice, the emperor's tomb,
a rendezvous at the other end of the Métro tunnels.

Here in the Luxembourg Gardens
the early dusk is like a slow dance
when day and night are in each other's arms.

Galilee

Everywhere we looked we saw the burden
handed by God-the-father to God-the-son.
When we reached the Galilee shore
our day excursion was half over.
We were taken further, into Galilean hills
to a vantage point with a bird's eye view
where you said *Look,
a valley like the valleys of Wicklow.*
The lake itself was like an Irish lough.
With pasture to feed the good shepherd's flock,
the land was lush, not what we imagined
listening to the gospels with their reports
of loaves and fishes multiplying, wind and water
staying calm when they received the order.
And those ten lepers, restored and cured
but only one of them returning to show gratitude.

No Infidels

The women of Jerusalem were out
fetching the Sabbath bread.
Our taxi-driver said he'd show us the King David Hotel,
before taking us up to the Garden of Gethsemane.

It was early in the morning, a day that commenced
with the scent of spices, with chilly temperatures.
At David's Citadel and Damascus Gate,
at the ancient wall that gathered in too many tribes for one place
we needed shade not from the sun
but from the religious fervours inundating us,
making us feel a sense of being *in medias res*.

Between peddlers of holy pictures
and sellers of essential oils
we moved along with the mobs: shrine to shrine,
sleepwalking the Way of the Cross,
climbing to the top of the Mount of Olives.
At the gate to the Temple the Arab boy blocking our entrance
smiled and said: *No infidels*.

A Different America

Angels in the architecture.
Diamonds on the soles of her shoes.
That's what the singer saw when he made

his American tunes.
Songs of a different America.
The horizons that Audubon scanned

for birds of the air, flowers of the land.
On all sides the many voices:
Whitman, Melville, Thomas Merton

in the solitude of his hermitage,
looking up at stars on the flag,
stars in the firmament.

And Frost's New England woods
with their groves of abundance.
The cities with their citadels and subways,

their heroes cast in bronze.
That's what the singer saw—
a different America, the one he turned

into vision-songs, folk-canticles
with the rhythm of calypso, boom-bang of jazz.
Songs to make us join the dance.

To Ludgate Hill

When we heard the heart-swell of hallelujahs
it was one of London's gospel choirs providing sound
for the *film noir* night-time of the city, the choreography
of the double-deckers passing through the West End.
In the underground we felt the touch of underground air,
the soothing gust on the escalator
descending slowly, the way confetti falls on a bride.
When we glanced across the river's wide and greenish
tint at what the Masters of Proportion built
we saw before us the gifts they left,
and imagined a morning there, on Ludgate Hill:
John Donne carrying pages of wet ink.

Seen and Heard

1. Georgia O'Keeffe at IMMA

I am here with the gazers, here to keep
an appointment with the flowers
of Georgia O'Keeffe: her long-necked lilies,
her cups of nectar. Oak-leaf, iris;
sunny walls and patio silence.
Or those cow-skulls the desert collected
on the ghost ranches of New Mexico.

Among her colours of abstraction
I sense the hand that turned to art
the bones of cattle; the barn and chapel.
Those night bloomers and wild petunias.
The stark horizon of the plain
that is everywhere incandescent
and brimming with the absence of rain.

2. *Leonard Cohen at IMMA*

Through a break in the clouds, the moon
was naked and, for the occasion,
the summer night put on its fragrance.
They came to hear this poet sing
songs of love and lamentation.
Three roses for the backing chorus
he picked from the roses at his feet.

He went down on his knees for a hymn to Eros,
an ode to the beauty of his soul-sisters.
That tune of his with the marching beat
and his epic Hallelujahs still echo
in the neighbourhood with the anthem
and the waltz we kept humming when he was gone
back to Boogie Street and his *Tower of Song*.

My Father's Hat

to the memory of Jim Greeley, friend of my youth

Dear friend, you sent me a photograph,
a black-and-white freeze-frame image of the past.
In it I am wearing my father's hat.
The brown hat that smelled of ancient sweat
and Dublin drizzle. The kind of hat
worn by Alan Ladd in gangster films.

I am wearing my father's hat
and I am seated between two companions:
together we are tightly bunched
like veterans from an old brigade.
Since then we have lost touch.
And I will never again find my father's hat.
It is hard enough to find my father in the old part
of the cemetery where all paths look the same.

Elegy for James

Baudelaire's forest of symbols.
A lakeshore in the American Midwest.
Wherever you went you were keeper of the scrolls,
an un-laurelled Dionysus. It was always the hour
when liturgies commence and the jukebox polkas.

Now we lay you down, ignoring the rain
with its misty exhalations, it drizzly haze
over your Blue Mountain, your Vale of Avoca.
We ignore the rain, those of us who form the final circle
with you in the centre, holding our attention
much the same as back in the day on Harry Street,
the local Parnassus, the harem of mystics and poets,
beer and whiskey on the round table,
and no end to the incantation of holy names.

to the memory of James Liddy

Fellini's Dreams

Fellini recorded his dreams
in sketch books and diaries.
Dreams in which he saw his obituary on the page
and made love to glamorous Anita Ekberg.

On those warm nights of Roman heat
or when cool sea-breezes blew from the Adriatic
his sleep was haunted: he saw himself with Pasolini
walking into the unlit alley
or dancing with Fred and Ginger
through the cinemas of Rimini.

Fellini dreamed of more Hiroshimas
and falling among thieves.
His dreams appeared as allegories
in the shooting script for *Amarcord*:
the scene with the ship strung with lanterns,
a floating carnival to light up the fascist years.

Ars Poetica

for Thomas McCarthy

To a poet ensconced in our Lisbon of the South,
I say this, write about the back lanes
of no importance, the hilly streets
where you like to walk on bright mornings.

Begin with a threnody for those who are gone:
the storyteller, the stone-carver,
the book-lender who passed on
The Love Songs of Connaught
to a boy listening to hear what stirred
in the stone-walled demesne.

Describe the evenings of rapport between
the apprentice and his patron: the fiction-maker
too old to care about good behaviour.
In fragments of lyrical candour
give us back the hero, the patriot:
his aura of rectitude, inference of danger.
He who in a time of brooding found the alchemy he needed
to formulate a Book of Virtues for the nation.

Tomorrow's Stanzas

i.m. Francis Ledwidge

When the Easter ceremonies were done
he stopped awhile on Chapel Hill
with its two ways to turn,
and its straight-ahead small road that took him
through the bog hush and riverbank chill
where the Boyne was strong and fast at Swynnerton.

Later, where Aegean shores sparkled,
in the *Tent of Mars,* in the *muddy ranks*
he remembered that Sunday spin, pedalling
through the land of open doors, grassy banks—
the lanes where carts trundled carrying
the mysteries of the dung heap

and a blackbird was singing in the singing trees
between castle and cottage.
There he heard the song of the chicken roost,
found fox tracks down furrows of clay,
in the apple orchard, the midden of ashes,
on the page left blank for tomorrow's stanzas.

To a Genealogist

for Antoinette and Eugene Keenan

Behind the mountain, at the far end of the muddy lane,
under trees that catch the sun,
you go looking for ancestors, consanguinity,
wiping camouflage from tombstone names,
dust from ledgers that hoard the generations.

In hard winter, verdant spring
you go foraging in the old cemeteries
with their shrines of remembrance,
art of the stonemason lost now in ivy and thorn
and thickened knots of hazel.

In public records, on slabs of marble,
blocks of stone, wherever annals are written
or epitaph inscriptions, you follow the trail
to the family tree that contains all answers,
seek clues to kinship, bloodlines,
an ancestral story scattered in fragments.

Souvenirs of Hard Times

for Gerald Dawe and Dorothea Melvin

The boats in the bay with unclenched sails
are out beyond shelter, trusting the day.
In clothes too thin for March
we walk the granite pier of Asylum Harbour.
The sea is calm like brushstrokes on canvas.
Behind us, from the high centre of the town
crowds come down to the station
where the coast train stops and waits awhile,
all doors open for exit and entry.
Off-shore, in a different light,
the ferry sailing to Albion
picks up speed on the spring tide.
By the water's edge, by sand and rock
we sense the homesickness of the departed.
This is the voyage they have chosen
while we turn back to the shuffling throng,
the rank-and-file on their errands—
going with empties to the bottle bank,
to the charity shop on their treasure hunt
for souvenirs of hard times.

SELECTED POEMS

1

Today is Not Enough

Today is not enough
to remember forever this summer,
strolling late across emptied meadows
and the tumbledown yard.

How sinister the motionless grass
and the single bush of blackberries.
The cowshed smelling vaguely of warm dung
on this voiceless afternoon.

Wilkinstown, August 1969

Evensong

From the door I saw unending distance,
crossroads where nothing happened.
It seemed like the age before cars.

The comforting noise of milk filling a bucket
came from the shadow world.
It was milking time in the country,
the hour I loved. Darkness crowded the henhouse.
I was afraid to enter. The bolt was drawn
to guard against the prowling vixen.

Yard

1

Two willow trees with towering peaks
stand with aged roots deep in the earth.
A zinc bucket rattles the wind.
And billowing like a length of silk
a nettlebed crowns the golden dungheap.

It seems strange to stand again
in the milking-shed with the empty manger,
dusting down the haymaker's
ball of twine, a whetstone half-erased
and the scythe still sharp. Nothing stirs
but the treetops brimming with heaven's breeze.
Rain in the rain-barrel evaporates
under the eaves in the noonday yard.

2

Once every summer he came, the knife-sharpener
encumbered with all the tools of his trade:
the whetstone like a stiff tongue,
the grinding-wheel to ignite sparks on the blade.

From over the railway line, he came to practice
his craft in grandmother's yard.
First he'd spit into the vessel his cupped hands made,
then rub them together, a kind of ritual gesture

before he honed the metals of the sickle, the scythe,
the cudgel; made them unsafe to touch
and ready as ever to level the hay-patch
down to its stubble, down to the last vestige of summer.

Childhood House

Grandmother in her black shawl
was stooped and barely visible
through the vapours of her kitchen.
In that kitchen everything shone:

linoleum, china, the stacked dresser.
Smoke discoloured the wall it clung to,
turfsmoke that vanished
up through the chimney and put us to sleep.

Grandmother—in her eggwoman's apron—
had a deep distrust of electricity.
With great patience she combed the hair
falling to her shoulders.

Late at night,
dance music rose up from the wooden radio.
The fire sank back to cinders and ash,
enough to keep the chill outside
in the crevices and treetops,
in the star-clusters of the clear night.

Dollars

Grandmother never allowed the electric in
because it was that fearful thing
that killed her son in America.

The boy who sent back dollar bills,
who in his stiff white collar
and antique tweeds looked down on us
from the cherrywood frame,
his place of honour.

Grandmother became a book
of bewilderment after the bad news
appeared in the long-distance telegram,
a message that remained for years

on the big open dresser
with its rows of cups, like commas;
its brimming jugs with rustic scenes.
And higher up on the dresser's peaks
she kept the dollars out of reach.

Smokehouse

The remembered day is over and it has left
the aroma of smoke in your closed house
and something else: the absolute stillness
of empty chairs and iron beds.

One room is laden with clothing
from decades you could never let go of—
winter coats, summer dresses;
pockets smelling of pinecones and hen-feathers.

The fire that burned through summers past
has petered out, gone to ash.
Soot has settled on the dresser's hanging cups
and glazed mosaic of plates and jugs.

Hallowed with age, everything remains in place:
drawers and boxes stashed with clutter,
the small window of wonder
that frames the good light and the wintry dark.

The Black Kettle Singing

According to the custom of the house
I stopped at the threshold and called out
before entering the den with its peatsmoke
and smell of newly-split wood.

The fireside matriarch: old-timer, forebear
tapping her stick on the stone floor,
told me all she knew by heart,
all she could remember

while I said little or nothing at all.
Her hands like fossils were raw from the drill
of pulling cabbage stalks
or knocking clay from potato skin.

In the half-light, in her corner
she had all the room she needed,
holding court or dazed by sleep.
Close enough to hear the black kettle singing.

The Old Life

1

Down the lane, astray from the main roads
it is like a place in the earliest folklore.
The walls of the tenantless house
are moribund, neighbours know
by divination the weather of tomorrow.

With lungs full of straw,
the scarecrow keeps vigil on what remains:
the stubble in the cornfield,
the traintrack pinned to the earth.

Older than the Old Testament
are the bones of the ravaged elm—
the tree in the garden
mixing its roots with the roots of the homestead.

2

Here an ancestor dwelt, thinking of the life he lived:
days of toil then the Sabbath rest.
Since boyhood he carried jigs and reels in his head.

Now the feel of a dormant world,
heavy with dust, fills the shuttered cottage
that gave good shelter once.
I smell the mould that overshadows
things of the past: oil lamp, candlestick, kettle
as black as widow's weeds.

A spider runs from the keyhole,
thistles advance towards the moon.
I step on the ash of fire that withered forty years ago.
Here an ancestor dwelt close to the cock-crow
of morning, dipping his cup into shining water,
the froth of evening milk.

Daguerreotype

In the sepia tint of a daguerreotype
a group of ancestors stands
ghost-like, transfixed.
They pose for the camera in puritan black.
On a day in August perhaps?
The women wear bonnets
and the man a silver moustache.

This is an interval
during which he puts down his scythe
but is thinking how long
it will take to get back to the harvest,
away from the household,
the women and children
taking a break from the life they inhabit,
one they'll leave vacant
for those coming after them.

Hen Woman

You cross yourself when you're told
that fork lightning scorched a man
in the next parish, left a wall scarred
and made a silhouette of straw and stone.

After the downpour soft ground is cooking
in the sun, rainwater floats on cold enamel.
Your apron pockets fatten with eggs
collected from haystack and dunghill.

Balancing unspilled water in two buckets
filled to the brim is a trick learned in youth:
you perform it well,
your knuckles turning to the colour of iodine.

In shadows of furniture you are left
remembering that the meek shall inherit the earth.
It's a strange world of right and wrong.
Gold wears off the rim of the cup you drink from.

Squeeze Box

>   *i.m. Paddy Traynor*

With his turf-cutter's strength
he shook melodies from the accordion:
old time waltzes and céilí storms,

the quickstep, the foxtrot.
Music that brought speed to his fingers
and sweat to his forehead.

The squeezebox held in reverie
has been silent since it crossed
the Irish Sea, home from the dance halls

of nineteen-fifties England,
land of the homesick,
a place he called *Over Beyond*

Arcadia

Here in Padraic Colum's drover's Eden
on the road between the Hill of Tara
and the birthplace of our most famous harper

I am surrounded by the earthly and the invisible:
the music of forever swaying the trees,
the winter robin in winter ditches.

In the solstice chamber light is visible
only for a while. Christmas frost is silvering
the cycle ways, the birch wood and the railway line.

I cross and cross again a bridge upon the Boyne.
There is true calm in the way the river flows
step by step on the river stones.

I am standing in a painter's scene:
the tinge of russet, winter's glass-clear air.
I am listening to the song that brought me where

green pastures became my Arcadia.

Ancestral Place

Leaving the drumlins
for the ploughland of Meath
we passed on the way the ancestral place.
The green gate, the roof
that needs mending if it is to be saved.

Roof of straw, house at the cross.
Rusting spade, rusting fork.
Worms in the wood
of the ladder that reached to the top
of the haycock with its wide summer girth
and scattering seed.

From the chimney breast
that held it for years soot falls,
ascending like wrath.
Forgotten grass grows in the yard
where we built a pyre
of blankets, bedsheets, aprons, oilcloth:

possessions that reeked
of damp bottom drawers
and the quotidian heat of the big open fire
that was constant but changed
from summer furnace to winter cradle.

Dreamsong

The dead from family photographs
appeared again in a dream I had.
Not everyone, just those from the farm
wanting their old lives back.

In the dream I saw again the boy I was
that boyhood August
with grandmother feeding the calves
and strolling the yard, her strong arms
holding ingots of turf,
her hair pinned up in an old woman's bun.

The half-door on its hinges
sagged and screeched. The hens
were going asleep in their beds of straw,
their safehouse of feathers and shit.

Under the Bridget's Cross
she hummed her Hail Marys,
conjured butter from buttermilk.
Then wrapped it in a muslin cloth.

2

April Love Poem

Into her arms I stray
like a fortune teller's prediction.
Two voices singing as one
ebb away on the words
April Come She Will.

Striptease. Tower of Strength.
fluent in the ways of saying her name
I step into this moment
again and again. This most secret place
where secrets are safe.

The Forty Steps

The randomness of things we look back at:
our younger selves, you hugging the cold
in a cheese-cloth dress, or running down
the Forty Steps of the medieval passage-way.

Behind the terraced houses, the dandelion yards
our love seat was a broken wall, a lintel kept us dry.
We were whisperers along the unlit way,
where the drunkard, light-footed, empty-eyed
was sure to sing the last song of the night.

The randomness of things we look back at:
you telling me I hadn't the ghost of a chance
when we closed our eyes in a dance without music.
Or retracing our steps on Duke Street
where we once saw Borges who couldn't see you
with your hair hanging free, fairer then than now
and framing your face like Françoise Hardy.

Amsterdam

    for Pauline

Smoothing the creases in an old photograph
I see a face like yours, a face like mine:
the two of us, nestled close
in leather sandals and light clothes,
stopped on our way through Amsterdam
where we crossed many bridges
in search of Ann Frank's timbered attic,
the tempestuous colours of Van Gogh.

There was no room in those narrow streets
of huckster stalls, narcotic scents.
Bicycle bells made heraldic chimes between canals
and courtyards bearing the scars of wartime.
In an unremembered place we stopped to smile
for the street-photographer whose camera
was unpitying and rendered us as visitants
of summer, two orphans in a fairy tale.

You And I

> *Now I am no longer I, and you are not you.*
> —Yehuda Amichai

That old keepsake of yours, the troll-face
doll stares at me from across the room.
I am in its gaze, unable to avoid the wicked grin.

The heating system makes cooling down-noises.
We doze and dream. There is no connection
between the dream and what happens in life.

The drumbeat of rain on the roof
keeps a steady rhythm, like afterhours music.
Soon the gale will be everywhere—

it can pass through the eye of a needle
or move heaven nearer to earth.
Once more the quieter sounds strive to be heard:

skinflakes dropping, soapy water dripping
from dresses and shirts. We lie still expecting a pause
in the movement that carries life forward.

Comforter

She presses her breasts to streaming tears.
Once again she's a child's comforter

washing blood and dirt from scraped knees
or soothing a nervous imagination
awake at night in the silent house.

She is the story-teller, the water-carrier
who is never more serious than when she's looking
for a lost splinter in the palm of a hand

or turning the cool underside of a pillow
towards cheeks inflamed by childhood fevers.

Dedications

> *They melt from us, our sons.*
> —Derek Walcott

SUNDAY CHILD, *for Karl*

It is thirty years since you came among us—
a Sunday child, wilful in the night.
One morning, just as stars were fading out of sight,

I came home to find you fumbling with first words.
Standing in your cot, wondering why the world
was unresponsive to your cries of mirth.

PHOENIX PARK, *for Simon*

Like an astronomer looking for new stars
you peered into the zenith of green branches.
Not even a handful of chestnuts
was left after the marauding early thief.

The deer watching from soaked grass
were statues imitating stillness and grief.
The stag's breath seemed inexhaustible
after his gallop in front of the wind.

In the empty pavilion and down by the pond
you were the explorer, making no discovery
until you noticed the corpse of the swan
dead in the water, making the water ugly.

Surrender

Your old dress of full-length chiffon
hangs like the ghost of Emily Dickinson
looking forlorn in our backroom.

The room is one we seldom enter.
It prompts memories of an evening
at the proms, a day in Ravenna.

It is here that we consign
to the rag-heap and the jumble pile
your glamour frocks, my tweeds

as thick as body-armour.
The straw hat that has travelled far
is there in the closet of wooden

hangers, hems unravelling;
and the baggy jacket, some buttons gone:
once it was fashionable,

now it is dated like the Aran-shawl
and the shirt with flounces,
frayed like a flag of surrender.

Cool of the Day

It was an evening for the mowing of lawns,
the clipping of hedgerows.
Not staying indoors
with the soap opera, the idiots' quiz
or watching CNN
for news of the next apocalypse.

My companion was sitting in bluejeans,
in the walled garden,
sipping a wine of Burgundy
that was close to a menstrual colour,
enjoying the best weather in weeks,
the indolent heat of an Indian summer.

Her face has always been the iconography
of my best dreams: my gladness,
my rapture, my golden apple.
In the walled garden she was chatting away,
her necklace of pearls—
the mother-to-daughter heirloom she wears—
as cool as the cool of the day.

Last Star Smouldering

It was one of those dawns
at the end of April,
on a road where old farms disappeared
under concrete and cement.
On the high-tension cables
there were pearls of wetness after rain.
An early freshness in the rinsed-out air.

I was coming home to the suburb on the hill:
Pasture-land where new families
settled back to back.
The first cough of the morning
could be heard through walls
in the cul-de-sac; then the stutter
of engine noise, a man off to earn his bread.

From the places where they spent
the night, sparrows flew—
diminutive and transient.
I was coming home to sanctuary and fortress.
Milk on the doorstep,
the last star smouldering.

Everyday Life

1

The heart-sighs of letters gust through the letterbox.
Our children on the doorstep chant farewell—
together they are going back to books
that lead them forward.
Wintersmoke broods over the rooftops.

Effortlessly all morning the dissonance of the kitchen
grows: a radio tosses rock music on the table,
the washing machine jolts its giddy load.

The housebound silence of the spare room
is rooted to serenity. Embers of the moon form
an eerie ghost-moon making a leisurely late departure.

A breeze that shakes and quivers
brushes the smell of sleep from pillowslips on the line.
You think you can hear the trickle
of a stream but it's water in the downpipe,
rain that falls a second time.

2

The radio-singers at night
were our nearest neighbours.
In the quiet we could hear
the reverberations of a feather falling.
On mornings when it was still dark
the effulgence of the bulb
was stark and painful.
Cups and saucers slammed on the table
woke me and drove me out of myself.

We came here in nest-building time.
Wind in the chimney was volatile,
milk turned sour after aging.
The cooker flared into four rings of flame.
Every noise was purposeful:
the stutter of the sewing machine,
the spin-dryer tossing
loose change left in a pocket.

Housewarming

For luck we brought a nugget of coal
and salt: the double talisman
to protect our four walls and fire-hearth.
The on-off switch bestowed electric light
that was all yours, all mine, all we had.

We were ankle-deep in builder's rubble,
dwellers of a bare house,
hammering nails and sweeping the dust,
making the space around us feel like home.

Bare wood cracked like knuckle-bone
when we crossed the floors
or climbed the stairs to take our places
side by side in the last sliver of dusk,
the first rays of the sun.

Vladimir Holan was Right...

Vladimir Holan was right:
the kitchen is the best place to be
with its coffee aroma, brewing tea,
prattle of the family and purr

of the icebox working its alchemy.
Stored away in its clammy shadows
are shining apples from Adam's garden,
cherries from Argentina.

A place of healing and mending
and clemency when we confess,
where the only empress is the empress
of wonders that never cease.

At the table of drawn-out pleasures,
wars were fought, you read my thoughts,
black headlines were passed between us.
It is here that daybreak makes its first appearance

and tenebrous evening through steamed windows.
Here that we have been talkative,
silent, amorous; pale as consommé,
rosy as ripe tomatoes.

A New Tenancy

Above the hall-door, stained-glass lettering
spells *Cranmore*:
the name suggests that long before
the marriage beds and cradles
a tree with bowers stood erect,
rustling where the house was built,
where eaves and attic came to exist.

The history of the house begins
in 1911: an English officer takes possession.
Moustachioed like Wilfred Owen,
he stood amid tasselled-fringes, war medals,
rooms crammed with the assemblage
of domesticity. Everything then
was still radiant, pristine:

brass and brick and balustrades
that split the late sun at evening
as it filtered through skylight glass,
window drapery. Eighty years later,
in the last decade of the century,
we came to peel back layers of paint,
to create a new tenancy.

3

All That is Left

All that is left of the medieval wall stands over
the underground river that snakes beneath
Fishamble, Cornmarket, Winetavern Street
where we strolled together like the pair in the legend
of Diarmuid and Gráinne or stopped to stand in
from the rain that fell on the ghosts of Hibernia.
The orators and the uncrowned king: all the fallen
who rose again on the stonemason's plinth.

In the Castle yard a tourist camera clicks, makes an image
of the gates through which the English departed.
In Ship Street walls were built on the bones of men.
Walls that listen to what the grey gulls tell.
The tourist can smell the lapidary damp
and puddled rain behind the Centre of Administration.

Return

Old haunts are best.
So you take the bus as far as the vestiges
of the city walls, the malt-and-barley district,
place of your first oracles.
To where the bells chime in the evening,
and bellringers ache in the Dean's cathedral.
Old haunts are best. The Forty Steps,
the tavern of shifting dust
where Napper Tandy plotted sedition.
The whiff of Liffey sediment,
risen from the riverbed, hangs over the market
of second-hand shoes, cast-off coats;
things discarded but still of use to the salvager.
In the office where our city fathers
fill the document baskets, the chill
goes out of the day. This is The Pale
and here are the keg-yards shut away
in the neighbourhood built on mud foundations.
It is where Lord Iveagh bestowed his favours:
the parks and gardens, red-brick mansions,
the bathhouse cold as Alaska.

T.K.'s Territory

Beyond Swift's hospital
and the grey slab wall,
down the lane where you remember
Paul Henry cottages,
it's all breeze-block and brick,
electric gates and double windows.

But this was once a sward
of city vegetation: blackberry fields
where you picked your way
through a rivery smell
and the smell of clay
shared with gull and pigeon.

Beyond Swift's hospital,
in the hollow glade,
on the hillpath like a pilgrim's walk,
it was late September,
summer's cadenza of final warmth.
There was shunting

in the distance: the evening train,
the departure whistle.
The hopstore harboured bitter grain.
In the cooperage a craft was dying
there among planks of wood,
hoops of iron.

Portobello Bridge

Twice a day I carry my soul over water.
The seedy canal blackened by car exhaust.
When first I came to the footbridge
at the lock, as a child
with fishing net and pinkeen pot,
it was through Little Jerusalem:
the avenues of exile,
past the synagogue that is now the mosque.

On the long road with dome
and campanile, steps to the doors
and life above the shops,
the town clock faces four ways at once,
chimneys sprout weeds
and windows reveal
lodging-rooms with lanterns
of papier-mâché.

Twice a day I cross the bridge
at Portobello, look to the hills
or leave them behind
in their morning glory beyond Rathmines.

Terra Cognita

In the shadow of the woodyard,
in the shelter of the childhood house
I heard the sounds of all the days:
sawblades, factory horn,
song of the delivery-man
who sometimes was
the neighbourhood's Good Samaritan.

The city then was a place of missing pieces,
gaps in the architecture,
generations falling faster than history.
The river—malodorous—ran its course
between the Four Courts
and the Franciscan chapel,
along the route they took
herding cattle to the North Wall
over ground that covered
memento mori, Norse-age dust,
street by street through streets that looked
beaten up, stripped bare.

Survivors

My father knew them, the master-brewers
of Rainsford Street who watched
and learned their father's trade
in malt and barley, hops and yeast.
Now they are gone with all their secrets
and old ways of tossing the grain.

My father knew them, the menders
of broken shoes, the brotherhood
of men with joiner's tools and the sailors
home from sea, who rose at noon.
Some were the forgotten of the Great War,
survivors who saw Edward Thomas's

Avenue without end. My father knew them
in their supping places, canal-barge pilots
who navigated the seven locks,
the newsboys of Inchicore and Kilmainham
whose evening mantra announced
the final score, the fall of nations.

Draper's Window

in Francis Street

There were armfuls of cloth in clear divisions:
cotton, linen, the new synthetics;
winding reams with curled-up edges
in the draper's window
and down the full length of the shop.

Fabrics of conspicuous and flamboyant colours
that would look good when cut
and stitched and pieced together
by women working the treadles and wheels
of Singer sewing machines.

It was a jumbled bazaar of curtain lace,
Communion veils. The cloth merchant
knew his trade: spotless white
for the soon-to-be-bride, lavender shades
for the widow tired of blacks and greys.

In the Bakery

for Ita Keating, and in memory of Phil Keating

I sliced the round fruit down to the core,
a tight knuckle that tasted sour.
Good hands lined with flour
were creating something beautiful
out of the dough, beating it flat.

Silence is golden, someone sang on the old radio
that used to fade and then come back.
It was almost a biblical task:
taking from the oven the abundance
of the baker's dozen: soda farls, apple tarts,
wheaten bread with a crust of thickness.

It was a place of sifting fingers
and measuring vessels, of work
that became a ritual when I filled
and emptied the kiln
or gathered up egg shells and apple skins.

Sam's Junkshop

for Peter Keating

In the tenebrous junkshop
he built a shrine to things tossed away.
A display of dross: the strange,
the familiar, mouth organ, jew's harp.

Like a character out of Isaac Bashevis Singer,
he stood in the doorway,
his bulk blocking the entrance to the muddle
of disowned and unwanted possessions.

Cooper and brass but mostly the poorer metals
of birdcages, clocks and kettles.
Keys no-one wanted, a bugle brought back
from the French Foreign Legion.

River Gulls and City Horses

1

Seeing for the first time Anna Livia
rivergulls made voodoo music.
They were restless over the city,
tangled in the hazy rain
or perched on the TV aerials
transmitting showtime at the Palladium.

They were idling above the dome
of the Church of Adam and Eve,
over the lying-in hospital where a lactating
daughter breastfeeds the new child in her arms.

Waiting to scavenge in the river's debris
they were haunting the Parish of St. Nicholas—
all the streets I wandered
as a child sent out for milk into the stargazers'
night of bliss where frost already hard had settled
on the graveyard of Huguenot families—
those weavers who came from France
with their looms and wine casks and need for sanctuary.

2

The animal had two faces,
one for the Sabbath and one for the workday.
His mask of sweat had eyeholes in it
with timorous eyes.

I was aged nine and trying to imagine
the weight that the horse dragged after him.
The coalman's dray was old and rickety,
the litany of the wheels was twice heard
in the echo-chamber of the street.

Children pretending to be horses
galloped with boxes trailing behind.
Later the boxes were chopped into sticks,
kindling for stoves that were lit
in the late coldness of spring.

Fifties Child

On Grafton Street in December
the Christmas lights sparkled.
In Woolworths, toy soldiers stood in ranks,
and snakes climbed ladders—all of them
a sight to the boy looking left and right,
up and down the aisle.

In the house where the war was fought
when the war was over,
in the rooms where cold linoleum
stuck to the soles of his feet, the Fifties child
stayed upstairs listening to the downstairs life,
to the smoker's cough, the belly laugh,
the deck of cards cut in half
by the hand that held the lucky number.

Those uncles with porter moustaches,
those aunts who rummaged in handbags,
lovers of singsong and Mario Lanza's
clear tenor arias—they whispered in voices
of sad disappointment and lived through years
that were always the end of an era.

Carnival

for Paul Doyle

Our no-man's land of broken glass
and stinging nettles changed appearance
to a fairground field
of carousel and coloured lights.

For seven end-of-childhood nights
the summer carnival came and pitched
on the patch of derelict ground
that was our El Dorado.

A guttural voice singing *Mack the Knife*
disturbed the women at Evening Devotions.
The Ferris wheel at unstoppable speed
raised our world; a waltz

with its tumult of horns and strings rang out
to fill the vacuum when the ghost train vanished.
This was our side-street music,
our merry dance in the grey alleys.

Picturehouse

In the picturehouse on Sunday,
with our lucky bags and ticket stubs,
we sat in the ranks of the hypnotised.
Those who believed in the divine
transfiguration of false idols.

All of us close together in a dark hush,
lulled by the first arpeggios
of a menacing theme. The plush red seats
made us kings and queens.
The projector beam was like light

from a beacon when the scalloped curtain
rose up or parted to reveal
a cinematic vista: Piccadilly and all its neon.
Tumbleweed rolling in tufts
down a lonely Main Street.

Mid-Century Sunday

In those days soon after mid-century
the dead air of Sunday was like a sedative.
It settled on the Dublin Mountains
and Garden of Remembrance.

The radio was a choice
between Dixieland, plainchant
or the shipping forecast told in snatches.
It was the day of darkest moods,
of rain as black as the Sunday prayerbook
and streets all silent

except for the marching band
whose tunes I loved
as much as their walk of righteousness:
the swagger in the way the musicians advanced
playing their anthem without looking back.

Postscript

The first of March, too soon
for any burst of skylarks,
too late to stop the executioner.
I have it in a photograph
taken with the Kodak,
a scene of sombre euphoria.
It was Monday and the sun was mostly
on one side of the street.
A gun-carriage wheeled
to the dead march of soldiers' feet.

They were bringing home the bones
of Roger Casement,
postscript to a nation's history.
For this last journey
he travelled slowly and travelled the length
of streets crowded with those assembled
for the quiet conclave of farewells:
women untangling rosary-knots,
broad-shouldered men,
heads bowed, arms crossed.

Written From Memory

> *How much of memory*
> *is imagination?*
> —Linda Pastan

The street we came from has disappeared
and the people too have vanished
into nostalgia, reminiscence, a lament for the past:
the milk-wagon, the baker's van,
the dull clang of a convent bell
striking twelve and six o'clock.
And the doleful Sundays with their
three-o'clock spill of men from the pub.
There was parleying on the corner,
small talk, racing tips. It was closing time,
the post-meridian hour of ease.
They were men who looked crumpled,
dressed in the livery of their Sunday wardrobe.
Sometimes they stood under the rain
with our fathers and uncles
arguing for hours about Cassius Clay.
Each of them wanting the last word
before going home to their soft armchairs.
Over dinner they'd say nothing.
Sometimes it was wise to be taciturn.

An Evening Walk in Maryland

When my father was a tired old man,
his pride in the Republic gone,
every evening he went for a walk in Maryland,
stood by the canal or stopped
at the dry fountain in James's Street.

By way of crumbling lane and convent wall,
gothic spire and brewery chimney,
he ambled as far as his last glimpse of the Liffey
before it disappeared to appear again
at Islandbridge and Chapelizod.

When my father became a tired old man,
coping with the scarcity of divine help,
each night he emptied his pocket of its hoard
of coins and his betting docket for the horse
and jockey that tumbled in the final furlong.

The Hot Bread of St. Catherine's

for Irene and Michael Smith

From Mount Brown and Golden Lane
they come to these streets
that are like the streets in an old engraving.
They have finished
the rubbing of brass, the scrubbing of steps.

A window brought to a shine reflects
mid-morning, the routine
of tradesman and apprentice,
of women wearing headscarves out to replenish
the message bag, the pension purse.

It's an old parish, an inner-city labyrinth.
And there beyond the shine of glass
are ribbons of meat hanging on hooks,
eggs in a basket, the cures
concocted by Mushatt the chemist,
the hot bread of St. Catherine's.

Hartmann's Camera

It was the year of *yeah, yeah, yeah*
and hair the length of Christ's.
The ambling horse,
a dray-nag pulling a laden cart
through the centre of the metropolis,
must have been one of the last.

In Erich Hartmann's snaps of Dublin 1964
I see again my father's city of lore:
small boats on the river
and people crossing the bridges,
all weary like the gravediggers
who have shovelled earth

for a burial in the boneyard.
I see again my father's city
of bad old days that were better by far.
Broken ground and jutting chimneys:
his whole universe that vanished
through the aperture of Hartmann's camera.

Eccles Street

It was the silver age of the sepia print.
From Eccles Street
the wanderer set out in the heat of June,
to take the epic route,

to make a day of small detours
with cronies in the meeting rooms
and hostelries.
Journey-man. Pilgrim. Tenant
of a creaky house

that after slow decline was gone in time,
I retrace your path
from the precinct of the dispossessed
to the dunes in Sandymount

and the round Martello with its climbing
steps and assonant echoes
that echo still, a hundred years since
Odysseus prowled his Dublin streets
and bawdy-house.

Songs in Sepia

to the memory of my mother and father

1

As bright as any apple in the orchards of Meath,
you arrived with crimson on your cheeks
and stood in a doorway afraid of the city
with its emblems and gestures: alien, strange—
the three brass balls above the moneylender's shop;
the river-silence, the hourly chime of the clocks.

In the heart of the city you were surprised
to find local variations of the stable and piggery,
the clip-clop of horses heavily laden with a tottering load
and the beautiful weeds growing beautifully
in laneways without any hawthorn or fuchsia.

2

I was beginning to grow a shadow,
to be able to reach and root in the pockets of his jacket.
It was strange and arcane that habit he had:

Doffing his hat, wandering everywhere but stopping
to let the world pass. I had to run to keep up
as he walked stiff-necked in his starched collar.

In retrospect I picture him taking a shave at the mirror
or mending things: nails he saved clasped
between his lips, a hammer clenched in his fist.

High Windows

Matchlight set the mantled gas purring.
A kettle's breath climbed the wall.
The world I knew was spectral: shadows grew
from the dumb congregation of coats in the hall.

From high windows I heard the ragman calling
and barrels tumbling into cellars.
My eyes drank in the gliding funeral,
the feast day procession: a whole street
coming to life and quietening down.

In the ill-lit buildings
with water running through them,
the voice of water crooned in the cisterns.
The atmosphere smelled of bronchitis medicine.
It was the atmosphere of the nineteen-fifties—
wardrobes, gas-stoves, fusty parlours
smelled of the decades dead inside them.

Family Lore

I

Under the beds, polished shoes
were waiting for the Sabbath.
The Singer sewing machine clickety-clacked
stitching folds of fabric.

Paint peeled back to reveal original colours,
knots in the wood. Up and up
to the top of the house rooms were filled
with the furniture and bric-a-brac
of those Edwardian years of marriage
when afternoons had an aura
of gravity that settled like dust
on the dressing table and the throne in front of it,
on decanters of glass and hunting scenes
that hung for years and hid the cracks.

II

Between the button jar and box of thread
the pin cushion bristled with needles and pins.
The books you read were put away
like folded wings. It is only days
but an age has passed since you were a boy
blowing out candles with your breath,
taking shelter in the sacred text you memorised.

The hard bed in the dark corner was your place to hide
when you listened to old stories told late at night:
family lore of hurts and quarrels, luck, adversity
whispered from memory in the parlour
with its Child of Prague, snow in a bottle, scent of lavender.

Shanty

My father's father,
known for his navigator's knowledge of the stars,
was filled with nostalgia
for ropeknots, anchor-chains,
arriving in the harbour from the night-pastures
of the sea. What he loved most
were the lights of the coast,
the seatowns issuing smoke
in wet November.

My father's father
knew the sea for what it was:
a proper bastard smirking in the darkness,
filling the fat pockets
of the harbour master.
Rising from his sailor's bed
his sixth sense told him not to trust
the complete stillness of dawns that felt
like the first day of the world.

Armistice

to the memory of Uncle Jack Smyth

In the days that followed Armistice
when the lamplighters returned to their lamps
and families convened to find out who was missing,
you came back to parlour songs, Zozimus ballads.

Home to your home ground, the Elysian city
where you sat in pub smoke, in the tight squeeze
of a snug, still in your greatcoat,
your three-quarter length shroud with mud on the hem.

Gas Mask

for Karl

Out in the shed with the rat poison and weed killer
the gas mask was sulking.
Its rubbery smell brought home from the trenches
was like someone's bad breath.

With its pig-snout it hung like a trophy
on the back of the door.
It had a scowl, a smirk, a look of evil
that could have been my own invention,

a trick of the mind when I was sent out
to bring in coal that was hard to gather
in the dark, in the panic to escape the sagging jaws,
the mask made of a grimace.

After Many Years

After many years I pass the house
where I was born.
A house of keepsakes kept in drawers.

The roof is gone, the floors ready to fall.
In the Stygian hall there is only the after-stillness
of the last tenant to leave.

It is nineteen fifty-nine.
The landlord climbs three flights of stairs
to collect the landlord's rent.

My father at the window,
half-erased by dusk, reads his evening paper
or *The Guns of Navarone.*

He sits until it is time to comb
his hair and step into the street
with his hat and coat and ironed handkerchief.

Finger-Writing on Window Dust

for Diarmaid Ó Muirithe

It's not that long ago
since the bell in the corridor
woke Andromeda,
and the tuning fork tapped on the table
made a sound that melted away.

In the school with ten tall rooms
I was caught once
finger-writing on window dust.
I sat with my slate and abacus
learning to fathom words,
listening to how the world was made.

The sibilance of Gaelic had a power of its own.
Ciunas settled us down
during the story of Moses
when Moses was found
in the basket of rushes.

A map of Africa showed us
where our pennies were going.
Out in the yard
it was knucklebone to knucklebone.

The Long Afternoon

for Al Cunningham

For years we lived with Caesar.
Virgil entered our souls.
Amo, amas, amat.
We pressed against a relic language
and it broke away in fragments.

In the company of Shakespeare,
his merchant Jew, his Scottish king,
we stumbled through a strange vernacular.
It was magpie season.
We gathered in equations, river-names,
the harm done by history.

With its sweet sickening smell
chalkdust floated over everything:
the wooden desks, the books of learning.
Through the long afternoons
we waited for the Bronze Age
and Renaissance to end.

The Wild Geese and the Brotherhood—
heroes with blood on their hands—
filled the foolscap page and taught us
a lesson in sacrifice, servitude, duty.

Riddles and Orisons

to the memory of Jack Hoey, teacher

Straight-backed, arms outflung.
In front of everyone
he stood like a singer about to sing
his favourite aria.
The dust of school-chalk
lay on his shoulders.

He read with both eyes closed,
brooded over Matthew Arnold
and Samuel Coleridge
during the last lesson of the day
when in a voice that was ceremonious
he created the atmosphere of the Lakes
just by saying *Windermere*.

Shakespeare, Yeats,
Father Hopkins, Soldier Ledwidge.
On afternoons when the glinting sun
came in or rain fell hard
on the window-ledge
he made their riddles and orisons
rise from the page.

Girl in Blue Denim

Denim-wrapped in jeans and jacket
she dances to the dissonance,
to Hendrix playing *Purple Haze*.
A Polish girl in Dublin, 1968.

She carries the weight of her faraway name
along with the lipstick and make-up
she uses in the search for love.
She is past the age of going home.

A girl alone among the living,
whose dark mascara makes her look
less girlish than she is,
less daughter-child than woman.

A Previous Life

From what sometimes seems
like a previous life, I remember
the stealth with which we said
Goodnight beneath St. Patrick's clock.

When I received your kiss
it was during the matinée in the dark:
the bicycle scene I think
in *Butch Cassidy and the Sundance Kid*.

Your kiss was then a healing art
after the dance, under the trees
on Clanbrassil Street,
the corner where in an ardent

trance we drew close
and I placed in your hands
the gospel of Pablo Neruda.
His twenty love poems and song of despair.

The Cana Inn

The law did not like the long hair
of the cider-drinkers, the ones who made the din
on Saturday night in The Cana Inn.

Not the one in Galilee, the Cana
of the wedding feast and the water-to-wine miracle.
But the one they later knocked to rubble

off Grafton Street. It was where we revelled:
carelessly dressed in denim and corduroy,
equipped with copies of Kerouac.

It was the end of summer, the waning
of another decade. The jukebox played
a voice with gravitas: it was Johnny Cash
singing *Girl from the North Country*.

Same Old Crowd

Once a year we gather to reminisce
on things that happened, things that didn't.
Together we are a reunion of shadows

huddled around a table of drinks;
the occasion on which again we are part
of the same old crowd.

Each is his own biographer,
each the maker of his own folklore and myth.
There is one who remembers

and one whose memories have been eclipsed
by disillusionment and the passage
of years since our initiations

in fellowship, high-spiritedness,
the antics of youth; since first we heard
Into the Mystic, slow-danced to *Hey Jude*.

4

The Solitary Life

I entered there
as if entering the Temple of Solomon
or a Tibetan monastery of silent prayer.

I went there, not once but often,
passing a morning or an evening in spring
where *Mnemosyne Lay in Dust*,

in Emily's Amherst, Homer's Ithaca.
Shoulder to shoulder with the poet who wrote
Save us from tears that have no healing.

On the reading table,
like a great inheritance, books that a match
could burn and turn to embers

were crammed with fictions,
crammed with fables,
crammed with the labours of the solitary life.

He Who Treads The Boards

> *There is a scene where he who treads the boards*
> *is artlessly rhetorical.*
> —Elizabeth Bishop

With his beguiling voice he has practiced cadence:
the whisper, the shout, change of tone
and change of pace: this actor
who hoards his accolades in a travelling bag.

A brooding Hamlet, a sonorous Vanya,
the blood vision in a Greek tragedy.
On the players' stage, soft-lit he makes entrances,
exits; the quick change from pathos to rage.

Master of silence and master of speech,
of the strut and the dying fall,
of anxiety, inertia and contradictions.

He is like a priest before his congregation,
this actor who must endure
judgments, opinions, the analogy with Narcissus.

Epiphany

Look! The orchard—
the boughs, the fruit.

Bright blossoms
part the still configuration
of trees in water.
Frost vivifies the moon.

Look! The clarity of gossamer
on bowing leaf.
Disconsolate flower
at the door of the tomb.

Comet

    for Sheila Wayman

It reappears in our garden of galaxies.
A soul in flight, a soul of ice and dust.
I imagine it, already there on the day
of the first man and the first woman.

And there in the time of Plato
centuries before Christ. It was nameless then
and nameless when in the season
of Roman festivals it was seen

by shepherds who watched for signs,
who were frightened by the celestial.
Now it returns to blind the new astronomers,
all the Galileos rummaging among the stars.

Two Stops on the Way to the Sea

1

In Drumcliff churchyard
where we stopped to find the epitaph,
it seemed just right that we were lost
in rain that pounded the car bonnet

and sounded like a horseman passing by,
his destination further on where sea-wreck
and sand-castle each cast a cracked shadow

and the ocean learned to dance like Crazy Jane
between the shores of here, there
and the island where John Synge
walked on air and heard the true vernacular.

2

He came to hid his face in Lissadell,
to empty himself and vanish from the world
of rag-and-bone merchants.

His poems were little stones
thrown to make a ripple. The trees with tree-light
made him think of the need for magic,

for the zodiac and occult.
Here he heard conjecture and philosophy,
the cooing dove and the crow's voice in the wood.

The fiddler played a tune out of folk memory,
a melody blown down from above.

Mangan

Fever-dazed he walks
through a sleepwalker's oblivion
and through the alleys calling
his *Dark Rosaleen.*

Black lanes consume the path
that takes him home
to crumbling brick and rancid room.

Pity him, poor poet
with a head full of words that rhyme,
who walks through his lost worlds between
Siberia and The Coombe.

And where he wanders
a steeple bell breathes on still air,
long syllables of sound
that follow him like a shrill
tormentor's song.

Homage to Hartnett

From Granada he brought back
Lorca's gipsy ballads.
When the blackbird whistled
in the school-hedge hedges
of Croom and Camas
he was there to listen, a naturalist,
a new and living Ó Rathaile.

In Kensington, on the underground
where nobody looks at anyone else
he looked ascetic
like a young Jean Paul Belmondo
as bony as the Rock of Skellig.

And on Leeson Street,
in the Saturday crowd he was there again,
raising a glass, striking a match:
the haiku-master of Emmet Road
wedged between Sweet Afton
and Woodbine smoke.

An Abstract Life

Sometime between the aurora and evening
the angel appeared
in Wallace Stevens' life.

Perhaps it was while reading
that he sensed the hand on his shoulder,
the hidden presence between words.

Whatever he sought he found
under the surface of his imagination:
the motions of clouds,
the fingerprints of rain that fell in the dark.

A man given to doubt who carried a prayer
then put it down on the blank page.
His preference for the fictive journey made him
a gatherer of places.

Poet of transience and erasure
who saw the rose turn to paper
and heard the serenade
of the man with the blue guitar.

Ezra

Ezra in the ape-enclosure,
a prisoner after the war,
smelling of soap that gives him
the fragrance of Casanova.

Counting his rations by candle-heat:
sugar, horse-meat, a ledger
in which to keep the alphabets
of east and west.

Ezra in the ape-enclosure,
his guard, a crewcut soldier
who does not know
the poet from the felon,

Cathay from Idaho.
Through the eye-hole
in his asylum door he hears Vivaldi
violins, the river-song of Li Po.

Hopkins

Wearing the blackest black
he arrived with a deep nostalgia
for the music of Henry Purcell.
He arrived by chance like windhover and skylark.

It was a kind of banishment
being sent to that other isle:
tea and bread in the cold Jansenist house,
wet days of summer

in the garrison town beyond the Curragh.
A place to languish,
to listen to horse-traffic
or silence in the noonday chapel.

He arrived from somewhere far,
perhaps where the South Star seemed to hang
or the wind of the valley
was dyed in the Blood of the Lamb.

Lorca

In search of the kiss that blooms
from a kiss on the cheeks
to a kiss on the lips,
you went in four directions
through the land of wounds
blessed and unblessed
through white villages
in the bliss of siesta
and grey dusk gathering in
the orange trees of Seville.

The time had come to place
the black armband
on your linen sleeve.
The writing on the page
got smaller, thinner:
a procession of words
you carried south
through olive groves
and arabesque streets
to Granada where the stones
were simmering in the heat
and flowers were withering
to ghost-flowers
in Manuel de Falla's house.

Georg Trakl

> *As a young man he had once been in Heaven.*
> —Elsa Lasker-Schüler

Somewhere on my shelf of metaphors
your poems are yellowing with age.
A heap of them like strange dreams.

They bear a mark where I cradled them for years.
Somewhere between your elsewhere world
and the battleline of bandaged heads,

you witnessed The Last Days,
the horsemen galloping in the rain.
Tired beyond belief, you longed for levitation
on the angel wings of sweet cocaine.

Lives of the Artists

El Greco

From Alpha to Omega his Greek books
were his books of revelation, the spirit that moved him,
marked him, made him *El Greco*.
When he took the road from Toledo to Madrid,
he enjoyed the journey more than the sojourn:
the places of rest, the towns on the Tagus
that offered bread or where he was guest of those
whose plain sharp faces appeared again in portraits
of Saint Jerome emaciated or Anthony of Padua
lost in a trance like a river-gazing fisherman.

Van Gogh

With all your strength you kindled
and quenched the starry night,
mixed the pigments it took to paint
the world you knew: standing corn, potato-eater,
sower, reaper and Gauguin's chair
pencil-sketched while you were oblivious of all else.
Each self-portrait shows you
in repose and dying a little
or sometimes sick with longing
for a new life away from sunflower and cypress.

Bonnard

Like a dappled Ophelia she lies in her bath
as a young bride, as a matron at the end of her life.
His first love, his last love, the woman
who was Bonnard's wife stands shaded by shutters
or doused in light streaked in to glaze the salon chairs,
the table arranged for a breakfast of colours.
It never ceased—the flamboyant, the subdued
courtship of the artist and the muse
whose likeness never changed but stayed the same
with poise, with insouciance.

Rouault

> *…always the same slut and the same clown.*
> —Leon Bloy

The charm of a whore's face brightly lit by rouge.
Verlaine, rueful in old age.
These are your subjects: tragedy, mischance,
the bad world fallen from grace.
A clown becomes an icon of the melancholy
dreamed up for man alone.
With angry brushstrokes you depict
the bone structure of Christ,
the immutable black and white of his sorrows.

Rothko

Alchemist, whose sombre days and days of luminance
filled the canvas and filled it endlessly.
It's as if a thief had taken your thoughts,
leaving only the stillness of what is lost,
what is gone. A whole life you gave
painting the intimacy between colours:
the vivid, the wintry, the sunblood of evening
and the variables of black
that bloom and fade like a bruise.

Night in St. Cloud

after Edvard Munch

The dead come back in dreams, they knock
and enter the nuptial chamber, the upstairs rooms
where precious things are kept—
Christening robes, glass from Venice.

The dead come back in dreams,
sometimes clearly, sometimes obliquely
like the figure in a family photograph,
on the margin, out-of focus,
never claimed as *one of us*

or the man in shadow in Edvard Munch's
Night in St. Cloud, looking out
at whatever pageant is passing by
or at the crepuscule, the evening lull
after the hours of the day,
the deeds that cannot be undone.

Club Nocturne

1

Billy and Lester, born to bend and break together,
to fall as easily as petals from her white gardenia.

Melancholy, heartache, solitude.
The litany of disconsolate jazz soothes and lacerates.

Sad troubadour, singing for the joy of it,
amid the blare of trumpet and saxophone:
that plague of locusts going straight for the heart.

2

He disappears into a tempo,
improvising the pace on tightened skin.
Like a weaver weaving lace
his hands are everywhere at once,
rooting out an old rhythm of praise,
beating a drum: his work-stained bass.

He is a man possessed, on a victory march.
When the current running through his fingers
starts to connect, there's a cadence
that goes from whisper to tempest,
that blows the Walls of Jericho down.

3

Miles Davis in his mourning suit, the master of synthesis.
In the monochrome era of jazz,
in Club Nocturne, he stands and delivers
a ballad to the most beautiful woman he's ever seen.

Soloist on his feet, the last trumpet blowing.
With his glow-in-the-dark cigarette
he leans back in his own sweet rhapsody:
the shimmy of *Autumn Leaves*.

Miles Davis in the years of his bad medicine;
an Orpheus with shoulder-length tresses,
curled fingers dexterous as they shift in a dance
or build a song of stillness in unison with the sax.

Whiskey Bar on Moonlight Drive

for Simon

The organ chant, the chiming guitar.
His all-American electric voice
always sounding like it's coming from

a whiskey bar on Moonlight Drive,
the canyons of LA.
Sometimes for old time's sake

we still play those Sixties songs
that outlived the singer
who died in the City of Light.

A god in tight leather
and unbuttoned shirt.
A Chatterton whose short life

was animate or still
depending on which song he sang,
which slow chorale, which furious refrain.

Golden Lane

Born beneath cathedral bells,
he heard their morning and evening *Pathetique*.
The cheerfulness of their clanging metals
came gusting to his doorstep.

The boy from Golden Lane
with an ear for melancholy.
The idol of Paris, Vienna, St. Petersburg.
The pensive maker of the transcendent nocturne.

Moscow congratulated him
for his lullabies to soothe the nineteenth century.
Night after night the privileged and prosperous
came to hear and applaud

John Field who made piano-chords
sound like the rise and fall of breath,
who when he played seemed to bend
and whisper to his easeful melody.

Visiting Chopin's Heart

At the end of his life he called for
a cup of Pyrenees water
to cleanse his heart, prepare it for
its final prelude: the homecoming to Warsaw,
a city built from ruins
and in the middle of it Chopin's heart.

The rest of Chopin lies in Père Lachaise,
beside Michel Petrucciani,
another pianist, whose night-prayer was jazz:
the dusky ballads.

Chopin the émigré never forgot
the grandfather clock that let time pass
more slowly; or the spring thaw
in the woodland his father bought—
ice snapping in a short recital
of nocturne and sonata.

The Calling Angel

after Arvo Pärt

The silence is for those who listen.
Whatever is given
is taken away.

Like a foetal heartbeat
it is faint at first,
the low murmuring of the Miserere.

With its chorus for calming
or raising the dead,
the trance-canticle levitates us

with its sostenuto-long vibration.
It's as if time has left us waiting
for time to fade.

The solitary bell
sounds like a calling angel,
a stranger on earth.

Elysian Colours

after Tarkovsky's Andrei Rublev

The horseman on the Asian steed
appears like an evangelist.
Snow falling in a church
leaves a snow-white crust
on the shoulders of Andrei Rublev
stern in his cowl.

The Holy Fool wants to be a wife.
The great bell emits clangorous chimes
over the town of Vladimir.

The strangeness of it all: fires
in a frozen landscape,
the carnal jousts of St. John's Night.

The conversation with Theophanes
who called him to his side,
who taught him how to trace the first outline
and paint with Elysian colours
the Byzantine Christ.

St. Petersburg Triptych

1. Brother of Water and Sky

We came to hear vespers in a Northern latitude:
the great choir climbing the octaves,
to see quadrangles and clocks and night-clouds
flying like Elijah's chariot.

The day is never over, the night never dark,
not even the hour when all bridges rise
to let the river pageant pass,
the flotilla of tugboat, battleship, barge.

The Baltic amber is honeyed and opulent.
Every noise is the noise of the past drumming
on the gilded palaces, St. Isaac's and The Admiralty
Tower that Mandelstam described
as brother of water and sky.

2. Anna's Sanctuary

We find it through a hidden entrance:
the arboreal courtyard, Anna's sanctuary
of little rooms that still exhale
the atmosphere of Russia in the age
of forbidden truth.

In this, her church of premonitions,
the ink on her petitions
fades; a shrine is made
of the icon in the icon-corner,
the empty samovar.

And there in Napplebaum's
haunted image Cassandra lives.
Poet with the inward look of the savant,
the look she gives is stoic, chiselled,
black-rimmed beneath a Cleopatra fringe.

3. *In the War Memorial Museum*

In the war memorial museum
a morsel of bread is the centrepiece,
the ration preserved
in the cabinet of blessèd memories.

Watching the blurred documentary
I envisage a scene like Thebes or Thermopylae
or one of those etchings of imminence
from Goya's *Disasters of War*.

But first we notice the metronome
steady and constant as a constant vigil.
It is like the heart-monitor
sending its signal, keeping faint hope alive.

The doomsday book is open
at a page inscribed in *bas-relief*.
There's a violin that's shabby and broken,
with the fingerprints of Shostakovitch.

About the Wounds

i.m. Janos Pilinszky

In your sage head,
behind your unfeigned smile
there's someone back from the dead,
from Harbach and Ravensbrück—
who's seen the truth
and solved the mysteries
about the wounds of Passion Week,
about the cross but not the cross
worn as a piece of jewellery.

To a Latvian Poet

He stands like a sentinel.
His ruddy complexion and snow beard
make me think of Rembrandt's
ancient sitters.

He speaks quietly and we listen
to his early life: his seven winters
of exile from Riga for being in league
with the academy of treason.

But that was long ago
when the birds of Latvia refused to sing.
Today he is the honoured poet
who seeks not to be noticed

even when he is called by name
to step forward into the circle
to read a poem that lifts the veil
on his noble nature.

In Vilnius

They are all radiance, the brides of Vilnius.
It seems as if Saturday is one long wedding.
Brides stepping through the Gate of Dawn,

couples being photographed next to Mickiewicz
or under the sign for the road to Minsk.
They go slowly into the Church of St. Casimir

and into the long-standing edifice
where frescoes come back to life,
the church that Napoleon wanted to carry to Paris.
Instead he turned it into a bed for his horse-cavalry.

Jan Palach

We came to visit relics of the communist state
and found the most precious in a glass case.
A photograph of Jan Palach who died to light the dark.

Broody like Kafka, no laugher lines upon his face,
no foreknowledge of what would come to pass:
how a future of ordinary days would never be his,

the student martyr with the melancholy gaze,
the man-child in the photograph
who went where he had to go, into the conflagration
that sometimes is the only light we have.

Villa Florica

for Pádraig J. Daly

In the villa that evening
the birds in the ivy were full of *bonhomie*,
up in the minstrel gallery
warbling their benedictions,
whistling their hearts out.

In the dead heat the thunder shifted
from far beyond to close behind.
Enclosed by trees of great height
we were listening, attentive
to the poet from Lesbos

and the poet who intoned his Balkan elegy
for a homeland that had altered shape.
In the mansion they gave us
a place at the table:
the wine was served from cool carafes,

after that the soup and then the salad
of cucumber and tomatoes.
The dictator's name could not be mentioned
without a chill to break the enchantment,
a theatrical stir in the sylvan camouflage.

Sunday Morning in Romania

Beware of the dogs, they said.
The ones in packs
that roam the boulevards of Bucharest.
But it is the multitudes on their journey—
between one lost village and the next—
that jam the roads and turn them
into something carnivalesque.

A team of horses stops the traffic,
two of them like sleepwalkers
ambling forth in unison
close to the roadside grass.
Last night's wedding guests have gone
leaving a trace of havoc
in the celebration hall:
ashtrays brimming, bottles drained,
the circle broken where they danced the *hora*
as if to dance was all that mattered.

The silver churches dazzle heaven.
In the Sunday market
there is always one who walks ahead
of everyone else to rummage and haggle
and do the deal with the hawkers selling
craftwork, table-lace, watermelon.

Haunts

In statuary and monuments
their histories are chronicled.
The cities of Mozart the vagabond,
of ghetto and synagogue.

Cities we first saw
in grainy newsreels of war,
where red rooftops form the same horizon
Kepler saw when he looked out
hunting for creation.

Cities with bullet marks,
with bridges linking the polka and waltz,
with baroque silhouettes, streetlamps
making ghost-rain of the drizzle,
slow-moving phantoms of the trams.

Museum of Last Things

Where the trains arrived
there is a stillness you can watch
in the heat haze and in the snow rain.

It would be easy to say
that this is a place without nature,
but that would be wrong.

There is hair that lived on
when shaved from the head.
Anonymous tresses, braids and bobs

stored in the museum of last things
where nothing is forgotten.
Suitcases without luggage,

spectacle frames in a tangled knot.
A midden of possessions relinquished
like the last strength

of Maximilian Kolbe,
the last strength of those who entered
beneath the false promise.

Snapshots

for John F. Deane

One image shows the shards
of Kristallnacht, a boy not sure what
he's running to and running from.

In snapshots taken by history's witness
there is always a spectre
worn into the grain, into the moment:

The camp survivor, the famine nomad.
The skin-and-bone refugee
behind the barbed-wire fence

or the war-child naked on the Asian road:
a ballerina in a ballet of explosions.
One image shows the fires of Dresden,

another, from the torture-chamber,
is of a man whose corpse resembles
Mantegna's Christ.

Sagrada Familia

While masonry and mortar were forming
the acoustic, compounding the honeycomb
of the steeple, the white sheets
in the pauper's ward seemed cold to him.
Gaudi with his silver-bearded face,
his ascetic rules; a servant of the Lord
dying in the Santa Cruz hospital,
his fantasia composed but not complete:
its plaster dust falling upwards
through hallowed space that still awaits
finishing touches, a final blessing.
The builders build with the speed of a century.
They are adding another year to Sagrada Familia.

Celtic Landscape

I have passed through places of holiness
and witchcraft, rooms full of armour
preserved from the past.

A fine rain smudges the air
on hillsides worn smooth by pilgrim
and warrior. In cloister-ruins
congregations of grass worship the stars.
Stones and thistles hold down the horizon.

I am glad to find a world so different:
crags that are close to the next life,
a kingdom of lonesome animal tracks.

Bog cotton flutters making shadowy noise.
I see a cold sweat running down the mountains
and thorns in the sides of the ditches.

Cross of Moone

What startled us was the rattle of gridiron,
the gravel track twisting under the tyres.
We were driving east, clocking the distance.

Oozing in the heat of late afternoon
the black tar was viscous
on the motorway of our Iliad.

We were driving east but stopped off
at the Cross of Moone, symbol of the creed
of fatherland and mother-tongue.

It was one of the first of the last days of summer.
The tops of conifers brightened and dimmed
and filled with birds with only one song.

Song of innocence, prayer without words.
It was not the beginning and not the end
but the in-between time before Amen.

Glendalough

He found his way
to a place of imperturbable serenity,
a garden of roots and tendrils.
Glendalough where he rested
his body on fern and moss.

To ward off temptation
he stepped into the lake
until it rose to his knees, to the rope
around his waist.

It was his portal to God, his place
to stop and hear the wind
passing over the treetops,
carrying the rook and the crow.

Now in early October
in the twenty-first century
Glendalough remains as it always will be:
Kevin's bed, the tower, the cross.

The dead have their vaults,
the wind has its tree
in the garden of roots and tendrils,
fern and moss.

Boyne Tomb

They were proud of the wonders
they worked, the Boyne people
who built this mound,
who hauled kerb-stone and megalith
up to the higher ground.
This ancient mound was built
on an upland ridge, whereabouts
of the scribe whose hieroglyphs
are undecipherable still.

Until short days of advent
when the sun makes tracks
of quite exact illumination,
the souterrain is lit
by bare electric light
by which we see the way ahead
into the chamber of changeable truth,
empty like the sepulchre
we saw in Jerusalem.

Achill

Take the unmapped route, the road
that is barely a road,
neither straight nor smooth
out to the edge of the land,

to the rough wall and chicken-mesh
that form a compound
fencing in the wispy movements
of rat and mouse.

There are dark circles round
the eyes of the rooks.
They have moods
like the weather and the sea.

The nothing-to-lose look on the face
of the tree tells you
that out here you have to live
with the fog's flirting touches,

with the love-bites of saltwater wind.
The atmosphere creaks
like boats in the harbour
finding it hard to stay still.

Paperweight

The stone I use as a paperweight
was found on a seashore in Mayo,
summers ago when we drove on the coast
and came to a cove not named on the map
of the Four Provinces.
The stone has been with me since.
It is the size of a fist, hard as a kernel,
lethal enough for Cain to kill Abel.
An ocean gift to the Connaught wind,
it was shaped by many weathers
and worn down by millennia
like the mountain in Mayo that listens to prayers
and disappears sometimes into the rain.

The History of Fog

Nothing bothers the man who observes
the weather in Clew Bay,
the squalls, the lacquered haze.
The quick sketch he makes
is of seacliff, rockface, sky so low it touches
the turf-meadow, the white gables.

They live on a fault-line.
The people who know the history of fog,
whose tracks remain under the reek
and close to the duach.
Sea-hunters, bog-cutters,
those who lit the beacon for the lost

armada of musket men.
In the country of apparitions
a little gust becomes a gale
commodious enough to lift up
and carry away the Céide Fields
and famine village harboured in the glen.

Wonderland

1.

after Sean McSweeney

The artist paints the ephemeral haze
of a sky in the west, works the spell that makes
the wetland pool a window to the underearth.

The artist as eulogist scans the landscape,
its tones and tints: nimbus, spindrift,
the mountain slope of rock and stone.

Like *those dark trees* that Frost looked on
with worn-out eyes, the trees of Lissadell
are weather-beaten, Venetian red.

The artist needs to fill vast space
with bog-soil, shoreline, a native bloom
that leaves a native stain. The ground is rich,
damp with rain, the last ridge of light
blue as the welder's flame before it glimmers out.

2.

after Nick Miller

Snow when it falls is a snowy blanket
or like plumage on the scrawny branches.
It is a good landscape for hide-and-seek
in the cold shadows of whitethorn and maple.

Power line and telephone cable
catch the rain and let it fall on the gorged-on acres
of borderland, forsaken territory.
In this high country roads twist north
into mountains, into the corona of dense cloud.

The trees work up a chant of incantation
and sing to the lakes—Lough Arrow and Lough Gill.
The western gale leaves its razor scrapes.
It is a ragged landscape of watery illuminations—
a wonderland for the fisherman with patience.

Sea Pictures

We stayed in a house of sea pictures.
A house with a view of the sea itself,
of a pier that stood in the tides,

crumbling to nothing, in need of a Midas-touch.
Sometime we had on our backs a sunny breeze.
Sometimes a gale chased our heels.

The cottage doors were always open,
exhaling heat from kitchen fires,
allowing the long twilights in.

There were ships in bottles,
caps and coats hung to dry.
In summer weeks went by without the lamps

being filled with oil. The days were gradual
like the time required to forget a tragedy—
death by water, a disappearance on the horizon.

A fishing village, a lifeboat station:
in summer sandals we took the back roads
between those places,

down to the white strand
where a local Prospero walked his dog,
a terrier chasing a phantom stick.

Or down to the harbour with its oil stain
making a face of Jesus,
its safe haven vacated while the boats

were on the herring-fields or hauling in
the lobster creels that August when
my childish drawings were a homage to the sea.

Surrogate

She was good at remembering the genealogies
of the Harbour Road, of the cottages
with their eyes toward the Mountains of Mourne.

It was always during the month of the first
ripe blackberries. She roused me from the extra minutes
of second sleep. Then we took the shortcut

down to the summer sea, sand in our shoes
before we got there. Out beyond the tidemark line,
the track of shingle always shifting,

she was the lone swimmer or seemed to be.
Surrogate mother who told me saltwater was good
when I cut my finger or fell on my knees.

to the memory of Frances Smith

Flood

It must have happened while
my eyes were closed.
The river poured into the town.
The moon turned up the volume of the tides.

Soon sandbags were stacked
like the trench-defences
in *All Quiet On The Western Front.*
Floodwater burst into back alleys

and bits of ground where people
were born, lived, died.
It came through the hall where someone
was singing about *Apple Blossom Time.*

Like the fire in Alexandria,
it surpassed our understanding:
everything destroyed
or made unrecognisable:

books and boutique dresses;
the shopkeeper's supply of bread and cheese
and wine, his jars of honey
and the tailor's dummy
like a backstroke swimmer in the Nile.

Spirit of the Fireman

Stardust and Betelgeuse,
those beautiful names that smell
of smoke and embers, fire and water.

The wind is fanning flames
into a corner of the sky.
All is alight in a daybreak of blaze.

And burning in the ashes,
in the sparks that fly and fall
is the spirit of the fireman

who climbed his fireman's ladder
up steps that took him
to the scene of life ever-after.

In God's Ballroom

When you call from a timezone that is distant
you could be on the spice routes,
in the salt mines or some place that skipped
the Age of Enlightenment.

Perhaps you are the interloper
in a holy temple or on the outskirts
of a Third World shantytown
that yearns for justice.

But no, you are high on a mountain,
in God's ballroom
where there are nights of dancing
and many kisses under the mirror-ball
that blindingly dazzles tango-partners
and those who *cha-cha*.

Elegy For Caesar

What remains is vestigial: the colonnades,
the death-rooms of the poets.
Behind bronze doors the duties of the soul
are inscribed on vellum.
In Circus Maximus the chariot path
is ruin and dust: an elegy for Caesar
whose cameo face adorns frieze and mosaic.
From the mouth of the fountain
water gushes out crystalline from the aqueduct.

The halls of the catacomb go on forever—
tributaries of the dark,
where once they waited for the first epistle,
the second coming. The idols looking
towards the Appian Way have stood their ground
since the day of conqueror and slave,
oracle, epic and prophesies of perdition.

According to Matthew

Falling sparrows, camels passing
through the eye of a needle.
He speaks in metaphors and riddles.
He is a riddle, the Virgin's Son
who stands to pronounce the blunt one-liners
of the Sermon on the Mount:
Blessed are... Come follow me...

In *The Gospel According to Matthew*,
the version by Pasolini,
Christ the agitator hurries through Galilee
healing the stretcher-borne,
casting away the bread of stone
placed before him in temptation.

Christ in the temple speaks in livid gestures:
upending and taking apart
the tables and tills of the money-lenders.
He sits cross-legged to answer the questions
of potentate and plebeian, or with a stick writes
on the ground, defends the slut against the crowd
with a handful of words quite clear to everyone.

Interlude

Looking at thorn I think of the thorn-covered God.
I sit and listen—an insect is scratching the wall.
My wristwatch, ticking obstinately
sends out a sound like a clenched fist
hammering and hammering.

In the yard a bony chicken
is picking at patches of sunlight.
Implements of the fields are going rusty
where the wet weather touched them.

Today we are submerged in the requiem
music of Good Friday.
The tree with its back turned to the house
is tranquil, as if it were dead.
Tomorrow we'll be at each other's throats again.

Lough Derg

Years ago I spent a sleepless night
among sleepwalkers ready to renounce
the world, the flesh, the devil.

It was all Dantesque,
circling and circling the purgatorial beds
in the wet wind and chill from the lake,
to the chant of mingling strangers
ready to make a new beginning.

Black tea, black bread
was the sustenance we were given.
In the first light at five o'clock
the shore appeared out of the dark.
It made us think we were close to God
years ago on Lough Derg.

World Without End

Water locked in a frozen pond.
Time stopped in broken clocks.
Blood safe in the healing wound.
A toy forgotten in its box.

The doubt among the certainties.
A dance that ends too soon.
The aftermath of laughter
becomes a moment of doom.

The seed waiting for birth.
The dead entering the earth.
Opulence bursts in one hand,
another hand is dividing bread.

Creed Room

for Joe Breen and Pat O'Hara

To the creed room came the newsflash
that mutated into hot metal,
ink on the pages of *Revelation*.

Ricochets from the first shots
in a war of liberation, the silence of weapons
put down on the peace conference table.

First inklings of small earthquakes,
of the pitiless epidemic.
News of the world and reasons to lament

for the innocents crowded into makeshift
mortuaries, for the hostage kept
in a new Gethsemane.

To the creed room came narratives
from the Sea of Tranquillity
and the Red Sea shore.

From the frontline and Great Divide
came paragraphs naming places
never mentioned before:

the streets where executioners
gathered stones, where death-chants
conflated to a manic roar.

Daytime Sleeper

Curtain cloth blindfolds the house.
Hands of the clock move forward
with feebler and feebler effort.
The chimes are wearying at noon and midnight.

The pillow, white for tranquillity,
has been warmed by the sun that shines
too little or too much.
In the room of the daytime sleeper

the struggle against sleep waxes and wanes,
flowers grieve for their lost fragrance.
Bluebottles round uneaten fruit
are giddy with impatience.

Pink Roses Black

In light that lingers when light has gone
the clock on the wall
shows hands that seem to stop or crawl.
And the windows of the hospital
reflect a lunar calm.

Nightsmoke from the boiler house
swirls in muted agitation.
In a corner of the ward
geraniums bloom, the only sign
of a life not thwarted by lassitude.

Pale on the pillow—
lips like parchment, eyes half-open—
the sick child wakes after falling
through the deepness of space.

At midnight, when the youngest face
wears the oldest expression,
the dark is perfect, it paints
the pink roses black.

The Mirror Tent

for Eilish and Gerry

Some have arrived from the river's opposite
side, over the footsloggers' bridge.
Others made Homeric journeys
and crossed the earth. Now we are all here:
the giver of Allah's blessing, the apostle
and emissary of Christ's new testament.

Girls from the east move graciously.
Their colours make it a carnival evening.
There is a truce between all trades:
the singers who perform spiritual chant
and cabaret song; the piper who plays
from his repertoire, *Slievenamon*.

The maestro with his Arabian drum
beats out a rhythm for the tasselled dancer
shimmying and shaking her hips
so that all eyes are on her
and her doppelganger who slips from mirror
to mirror in the mirror-tent.

Poem Beginning with a Line from Raymond Carver

> *The days seemed to pass only to return
> again. Like a dream in which one thinks,
> I've already dreamt that.*
> —Raymond Carver

That line of Carver's
about *the lightning speed of the past*
reminds me it is two months since
I cut the dead branches
and bagged the leaves that came to the door.

Now it is time for fireworks that dance
in the first night sky of January.
The old year ends with the amity
of people in their glad-rags,
an interlude for love songs or laments

or the stroke of midnight
when bells, exhilarant,
seem to walk on air and leave behind
their echo for St. Brigid's Day, St. Valentine's.

Gifts

1. Gillette

We were not yet wideawake.
My morning skin against the nape
of your neck was rough and bristled—

like sandpaper, you said. So later
in the supermarket, along with other necessities,
you chose for me a gift of razor-blades,

shaving soap: then through the foam
the strokes of the thin steel
gave my face a glabrous, newborn patina.

2. Chanel

The bottle of fragrance
brought back from France
is waiting to be opened and daubed on
just under your ears
and at the base of your throat.

A familiar scent that leaves its trace
and stays when you're gone,
like a ghost in the wardrobe,
tangled in all your garments,
the silk of a blouse,
the wool of a winter cardigan.

Corrib

The day we sailed the Corrib
the lough behaved like a cosmic force,
capricious and primordial.

Our vessel swayed
like the vessel in the hands
of the potter who shapes the clay.

It all happened as suddenly
as the way we sometimes turn our lives.
With seeing-eyes you took it in:

the river bank appearing
and disappearing and then the lake,
a small expanse compared

to your Great Lakes of Michigan.
You stood on deck in heavy weather.
I stayed below in the circle of story-tellers.

There was no shelter, no anchorage.
No safe passage through thrashing spray
to Annaghdown,

the day we sailed the Corrib, upstream
to where the land became unseen
like the Land of Promise.

Nora Barnacle's House

I was looking for Nora Barnacle's house
but never found it.
Instead I saw her apparition in the water
with the Corrib swan,
the one leading the others forward,
the one with slender contours
eyeing the stranger on the riverbank
under the flowering tree.

I was looking for the house of Nora Barnacle
but wandered instead up the aisle
of the stone-walled cathedral,
where liturgical smoke lingered
after some ritual, after the sign of peace
when everyone leaves to go out
into the other world where first
their eyes adjust and then they see
the choppy Corrib, the swan in the water,
and between the branches of the tree
petals falling, settling
on the grassy bank beside the weir.

September Song

Autumn has come stripping the trees
to make them look like an army in defeat.
Soon everything will appear bereft,
even the girls on the street in décolletage
and canal swans nesting by the side of the bridge:
A pair of them in a swan-marriage,
schooled to be faithful companions.

Roads are brimming with slow-motion traffic
going out of the city, home to the foothills,
to time in the garden pulling weeds,
the Hollywood epic on late-night TV:
the one with the long list of etceteras
scrolled in haste before we turn over
in the double bed of brass reflections.

Free State

for John McGahern

Saying *Goodbye* at the airport
you speak of destinations far from home,
of distance that wearies
the jet age traveller
and the long journey ahead
through all the beautiful cities.
Cities like stories waiting to be read.

But I am happy
motoring through the Free State,
the Glebe Road where O'Carolan dragged his harp,
the hilly landscape where on some days
the lake is radiant and very still.
On other days it is like a page
of thumbprints, dull and marked
by cloud-shadow
and the meadow-dust of Leitrim.

Goldenbridge

In the year when years of bliss
were made extinct you stepped into the annals,
the histories of Goldenbridge.

In the name-book that assembled many Marys
your name was entered.
The itineraries of childhood you remembered
as days of slow duration
when your spirit was spirited away.

And so it was a childhood of learning
to keep silent, keep in line,
to turn the other cheek,
to quicken your steps on waxed floors
in a school without pity.

Leaving behind all you loved,
you stepped into the glimmer-world
of orphanage and sanatorium,
dormitory and TB room:
places so well hidden
they could have been the hidden half of the moon.

in memoriam Mary Isaacson (May Rice)

Aria

> *to the memory of Jerome Hynes*

Tears have a history of falling
Galway Kinnell says in his poem *Goodbye*.
But it was the history of a smile you taught us.
How it lives, how it dies.

We have just come from Vinegar Hill
to hear the opera singers sing,
alone and in unison, an autumnal aria
from *Lucia di Lammermoor*.

And we shall miss the way you stood,
dressed up, black suited, colour
on your cheeks in the doorway of the theatre
where you were ready to give your salute

and greeting, your handshake
that gripped each of us in turn
as we paraded one by one
into the audience waiting for the overture.

Elegy in March

to the memory of Francis Joly

You would not want an in memoriam poem, no elegy or song.
But your absence seems far-fetched and wrong.

The days with your name on them melt into air.
When you died it was the coldest of cold March weather,

the bare tree-tops were desolate, their choir-stalls empty
in this place that made you feel at home.

You had not finished reading the Russian scribes
or explaining Marx and Freud to those who'd listen.

For you last chance and lost chance were one,
a weight to carry like the gun on your shoulder

when you walked the hunting grounds and fields of clover
in this place that made you feel at home,

this broken province where hearts are head-strong,
where the best of our legends come from.

End of Story

Pictures of forefathers
who fought and died. Books from
a bookhive of common knowledge.

Today we watched the emptying out
of a house, the stripping down
of familial lives to a last inventory.

This assembly of poor man's riches
was masculine and feminine,
ornament and utensil.

The frame that fell and smashed
wedding-day smiles and looks,
a favourite chair, the table that became

the centre of the universe.
These are what the house clung to
as it stood for a century,

breathing out and breathing in.

Ovid in the Garden

The Gingko tree rising taller than the house it shades
bends just a little forward like a woman carrying water.
In urns of terracotta the good-for-nothing stalks
stand naked, last remnants of what-was:
marigolds, carnations, forget-me-nots.

The dead garden in its film of frost is chalk-white, utterly still.
The best place to bring the tablecloth and shake from it
the grains of salt, the food crumbs for the sparrows
in their sparrow-kingdom, the ones that seem to appear
for early morning matins, for the same half-hour each evening.

Among the leaf-skeletons let me be Ovid in the garden
waiting for the hanging baskets of high summer
to make their second coming,
and the first green shoots to spring
from ivy on the trellis, from the tired rhododendron.

Putting on the Grey Suit

for Dennis O'Driscoll

George Herbert wrote
of *the folly of distracted men.*
But often we forget
we will not pass this way again.

Putting on the grey suite
we are set in motion, *en route*
like the morning memo.

The keyboard is the juju
that we touch, the answer machine
a sentinel to watch over us.

Like clockwork we finish
and commence the days we circle
or mark with an X.

We write reports and pass away a life
as foot-soldiers making footnotes,
field-workers among the sheaves

counting down the office hours,
the middle years
until they reach the last hour

of exhaustion when
we close the ledger, put down the pen
and gather what we worked to earn.